THE
DO'S
AND
DONT'S
OF
MONEY

THE
DO'S
AND
DONT'S
OF
MONEY

Easy Solutions for Everyday Problems

SUZE ORMAN

HAY HOUSE, INC.

Carlsbad, California • New York City
London • Sydney • Johannesburg
Vancouver • Hong Kong • New Delhi

Published and distributed in the United States by: Hay House, Inc.: www
.hayhouse.com® • *Published and distributed in Australia by:* Hay House Australia Pty. Ltd.: www.hayhouse.com.au • *Published and distributed in the United Kingdom by:* Hay House UK, Ltd.: www.hayhouse.co.uk • *Published and
distributed in the Republic of South Africa by:* Hay House SA (Pty), Ltd.: www
.hayhouse.co.za • *Distributed in Canada by:* Raincoast Books: www.raincoast
.com • *Published in India by:* Hay House Publishers India: www.hayhouse.co.in

Book design: Charles McStravick

The PBS Logo is a registered trademark of the Public Broadcasting Service
and used with permission

Library of Congress Control Number: 2014931480

Tradepaper ISBN: 978-1-4019-4601-2

17 16 15 14   4 3 2 1
1st edition, March 2014

Printed in the United States of America

CONTENTS

INTRODUCTION

I know that you're busy. There is so much information out there about how to manage your money, so much conflicting advice, and so many options. How are you supposed to wade through it all to make the best decisions for yourself and your family?

That's where this book comes in. *The Do's and Don'ts of Money* is an easy-to-understand guide to help you navigate the major financial choices you'll make throughout your life. You'll learn the basics about financial security, credit scores, loans, mortgages, retirement, life insurance, and more. I make sure to explain the key parts of my advice, so that you're able to make an informed decision when the time comes.

My hope is that with this book as your reference guide, you will be empowered to make the most of your money.

Lay the Foundation
for
Financial Security

PART 1

BUILD AN EMERGENCY SAVINGS FUND

DO . . .

AIM TO SAVE EIGHT MONTHS OF LIVING COSTS IN AN EMERGENCY FUND.

I know that sounds like a lot. But you can and will do this. Don't worry, I don't expect you to snap your fingers and have eight months saved up pronto. I get that it will take time. But what's important is that you make it your goal to eventually set aside enough money so you could cover your living costs—food, rent/mortgage, utility bills, gas, insurance—for eight months. Why that long? Because as we saw during the last recession—and as we still see many people experiencing—it can take a long time to find a new job if you are laid off. Eight months = peace of mind.

DO . . .

KEEP YOUR EMERGENCY FUND AT A FEDERALLY INSURED BANK OR CREDIT UNION.

There is no better way to keep this important money absolutely safe than to keep it at a bank or credit union that is federally insured. If your emergency fund has less than $250,000 in it, you can rest easy. Even if something happened to the bank or credit union—and that's not common—the federal government will step in and make sure you get every penny back. Every penny, do you hear me?! For banks, you can check their front door or their website for a small decal or icon that says it is a member of the FDIC. That stands for Federal Deposit Insurance Corp. For a credit union, you want to look for a decal or icon that says it is a member of the NCUSIF. That stands for National Credit Union Share Insurance Fund.

DO . . .

AUTOMATE YOUR EMERGENCY SAVINGS.

Every bank and credit union will be happy to set up a system for free in which each month (or every two weeks, or once a quarter—it's up to you to set the frequency) it will automatically transfer money from your checking account into your savings account. This is the best way to save for any goal. Rather than have to rely on your good intentions to set the money aside, it's done for you. How much you have automatically transferred is up to you. I have a challenge for you: Think of a sum that you think you could handle saving each month. Okay . . . now increase it by 10%. Yes, I said 10%. I know you can do this. You must do this—for your and your family's security. Need ideas on where to come up with the money? Go to Part 4, Manage Spending, for my Do's and Don'ts on Spending.

DON'T . . .
INVEST YOUR EMERGENCY FUND IN THE STOCK MARKET.

An emergency fund needs to be 100% there for you at a moment's notice. When you invest in stocks you never know at any given point what it may be worth. Just think about if you had your emergency savings invested in stocks in 2008–2009 when the markets dropped more than 30%. If you had $25,000 set aside in your emergency savings in stocks, your emergency fund's value might have fallen to $15,000 or so. What if you lost your job then, and instead of having $25,000 to help you get through the tough time, you only had $15,000? A savings account at a federally insured bank or credit union is the best vehicle for your emergency savings. Don't worry if you aren't earning much interest right now. This isn't an investment. This is your safety cushion. Safety first!

DON'T . . .

ASSUME ANY ACCOUNT YOU HAVE AT A BANK OR CREDIT UNION IS "SAFE."

Okay I know that probably has you scratching your head after I just told you an account worth less than $250,000 would be safe at a federally insured bank or credit union. Here's the twist: classic bank savings accounts, certificates of deposits, and checking accounts are fully insured. But maybe you've noticed that your friendly bank and credit union also sells mutual funds, insurance, or other investments. Those accounts aren't insured. Only what are called *deposit accounts* are covered. If you buy a mutual fund or other investment through your bank or credit union, there is no guarantee that you will get 100% of your money (called your "prinicipal") back. It depends on the performance of the investment you chose. If you bought a stock mutual fund through a subsidiary of a bank or credit union, and stocks go through a rough patch, your fund's value will decline. Just because you bought it at a federally insured bank or credit union doesn't mean you are protected from market risk.

DON'T . . .

LOAN ANYONE MONEY IF IT WILL COME OUT OF YOUR EMERGENCY SAVINGS.

It is our natural instinct to want to help someone in need, especially if that someone is family or a dear friend. I get it, trust me. But here's what I need you to get: If you give (or loan) someone money from your emergency savings, you have just put yourself at risk if you no longer have an eight-month cushion. Helping isn't helping if it weakens *your* financial security.

PART 2

GET OUT OF CREDIT CARD DEBT

DO . . .
PAY THE MINIMUM DUE ON ALL CURRENT BILLS.

I know how overwhelming it can become if you are in credit card debt, and the bills start growing and you aren't sure what bill to tackle first. Always, always, always pay at least the minimum amount due on every current bill. And make sure that minimum payment arrives *on time*. This may surprise you, but being able to pay the minimum on time every month is the single largest factor in building and maintaining a solid credit score. (See Build a Strong Credit Score for more about this topic.)

DO . . .

TRY TO GET THE LOWEST POSSIBLE INTEREST RATES ON YOUR CARDS.

If you are paying a high interest rate on your credit cards and you have a good FICO score of at least 720, you might be able to talk your way into a lower interest rate. Call the credit card company and ask if they can do any better on the interest rate. If they don't budge, let them know your intention is to do a balance transfer to another card. The prospect of losing your business may prompt them to reconsider your rate-reduction request.

DO . . .

ALWAYS KEEP PAYING AT LEAST THE ORIGINAL MINIMUM DUE, EVERY MONTH.

Your credit card issuer recalculates your minimum payment due every month, based on your current balance. If you are paying down your balance that means the credit card will reset your minimum lower. Why? They want you to take more time to get out of debt, because it means you will end up paying more interest. Don't fall for this. Do not decrease your payment. Whatever your original minimum payment was, keep paying at least that much every subsequent month. For example, let's say your minimum payment due is $30 this month. Over time, as you reduce your balance, the minimum payment on your statement might say you must pay only $21. That's the trap! I want you to ignore the changing minimum and keep paying at least the $30 you paid the first month you set out to tackle your credit card balance.

DO ...
PAY *MORE THAN* THE MINIMUM ON YOUR HIGHEST-RATE CARD.

Once you've got your interest rates as low as possible, it's time to prioritize your payback plan if you have multiple cards with balances. Organize your statements starting with the card with the highest interest rate (first) to the card with the lowest interest rate (last). You are to pay the minimum amount due on every card, as I explained above. But I want you to send in *more than the minimum* on the credit card with the highest interest rate. How much higher? Again, I am going to challenge you. I want you to add the equivalent of 20% of all your outstanding debt on all your cards. So let's say your total balance due on all your cards is $500. Twenty percent of $500 is $100. So you are to add $100 to the minimum payment on your highest rate card. I know that may seem out of reach, but please try this for a few months. In Part 4, Manage Spending, you will find advice on how to "find" more money to put toward your goals.

Once the balance on the highest-rate card is paid off, add the entire amount you were paying each month on that card to the minimum payment on the card that now moves into the spot of "highest rate card with a balance."

Once the second card is paid off, move on to the third . . . and keep repeating this with every card.

At suzeorman.com you can use my free Debt Eliminator tool to help you tackle your credit card debt.

DO . . .

GET HELP FROM THE AICCCA OR THE NFCC.

If your credit card debt is too overwhelming, and you feel lost, contact the Association of Independent Consumer Credit Counseling Agencies (aiccca.org 866-703-8787) or the National Foundation for Credit Counseling (nfcc.org 800-388-2227). These are known as debt management companies, or as I call them, the "good guys" whose advice and help you can trust. Counselors certified by the AICCCA or the NFCC—both are non-profits—are focused on truly helping you.

DON'T . . .

FALL FOR A DEBT CONSOLIDATOR OR DEBT RELIEF COMPANY.

You've probably seen the late-night ads on television or heard a pitch on the radio for a company that promises to make your credit-card-debt problems disappear. Be very, very careful. Sadly, many companies that say they will negotiate deals with your credit card issuers are only focused on taking money from you. Any firm that asks for a big sum of money up front is not to be trusted. And as noted above, the best step is to contact the AICCCA or the NFCC and have them put you in contact with a legitimate credit counselor. The Federal Trade Commission—which deals with a lot of consumer complaints about debt consolidator scams— also recommends another layer of protection: check with your state Attorney General (you can find contact info at www.naag.org) to see if there are any complaints against a company you are considering working with, and also check with your local consumer-protection agency for any potential red flags (you can find contact info at www.usa.gov/directory/stateconsumer/index.shtml).

DON'T ...
AUTOMATICALLY CANCEL CREDIT CARDS.

After you've worked so hard to get out of credit card debt, it may seem like an act of strength and commitment to cancel your cards so you never get into debt again. Be careful about doing this. The best move is to tuck the cards away where you know you won't use them, but don't cancel them. As I will explain in Build a Strong Credit Score, your debt-to-credit-limit ratio (how much you owe on all your cards as a percentage of your total credit limit) is a major factor in determining your credit score. If you cancel your card, that means your credit limit will decrease and that can increase your debt-to-credit ratio, which would end up dinging your credit score.

If you are worried you will not have the self-control to avoid overspending on credit cards, that's an important truth to stand in. I get it. In that case, just cut up your cards so you cannot use them but don't cancel them (unless you are paying an annual fee). But make sure you maintain at least one credit card that you use regularly and pay off in full each month. This will help you build and maintain a good FICO score. If you had the strength and resolve to get out of debt, I am confident you have the strength and resolve to now spend responsibly, too.

PART 3

BUILD A STRONG CREDIT SCORE

DO ...

UNDERSTAND WHY A CREDIT SCORE IS SO IMPORTANT.

If you ever plan to buy a home with a mortgage or buy a car with a loan, or you want to open a cell phone account or a utility account without having to make a big deposit, you need a credit score. Plain and simple: your credit score is your financial report card that determines if you will be eligible for the best deals, and what terms (interest rate, down payments, deposits, etc.) you will be offered. Many landlords check credit scores as a part of the application process.

DO ...
FOCUS ON YOUR FICO CREDIT SCORES.

There are many companies that offer credit scores. Even if it is free (and many charge you plenty) your FICO credit score is the only score that really matters. Why? Because it's the credit score banks and lenders most often use when they are considering your application.

You actually have three FICO scores, one each from the three major credit bureaus: Equifax, Experian, and TransUnion. In early 2014 the typical cost is about $20 for each FICO score. But you can get your Equifax score for $4.95 if you sign up for a 30-day trial at myfico.com. Just be sure to cancel your account immediately after you get your score.

Unless you will soon be applying for a mortgage or car loan you don't need to get all three at once. If you are going to be applying for a loan, then I do think it makes sense to pay for the other two, just to make sure there are no surprises that could sink your loan application.

DO . . .

AIM FOR A FICO CREDIT SCORE
OF AT LEAST 720.

FICO credit scores range from 300–850. The higher your credit score, the better deals (lower interest rates on loans, for example) you will be offered. In fact, ever since the financial crisis, if you don't have a high credit score it can be very hard to get a mortgage, period. So what's very good? Anything above 720 is solid; and above 760 is even better. Don't worry about getting to 800 or higher. Life is too short to obsess about your credit score. Maintain a score in the range of 720–760 and you will be just fine.

DO . . .

CHECK YOUR FILE AT THE
CREDIT BUREAUS.

Your FICO credit score is calculated based on information compiled by each credit bureau. You have an Equifax credit report, an Experian credit report, and a TransUnion report and each of those files are then used to compute your three FICO scores. As you may have experienced or heard about, the credit bureaus sometimes have wrong information, or they fail to update your file. You are entitled to get one free credit report from each of the credit bureaus every year. The only place you should go to get your credit report is annualcreditreport.com. Going through annualcreditreport .com ensures you will not be asked to pay a penny to get your report. You can get all three reports at once. Another strategy is to get one report every four months. For example, request your Equifax report in January, Experian in May, and TransUnion in September. It's a free way to keep an eye on your credit reports throughout the year. Typically there is great overlap in the information each bureau has. And when you report an error (follow the instructions you will be provided when you get your report) the bureau you contact is required to share that information with the two other bureaus.

FICO SCORE BREAKDOWN

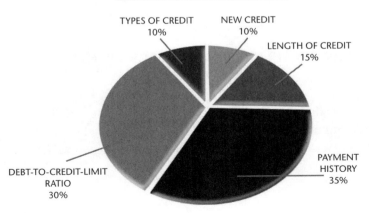

TYPES OF CREDIT
10%

NEW CREDIT
10%

LENGTH OF CREDIT
15%

PAYMENT HISTORY
35%

DEBT-TO-CREDIT-LIMIT RATIO
30%

DO . . .
USE A CREDIT CARD.

I am a huge believer in paying with cash; there's no better way to stay out of debt if you only spend what you have. But the reality is that you should also use a credit card a few times a month. Even if you love your debit card—and I am a big fan of debit cards—you also need to have and use a credit card. Your track record in making payments on your credit card plays a large role in determining your credit score. Payments on your debit card are not tracked for that purpose. Without at least one credit card account that is active and that you pay off in full each month, you will have a hard time building a great credit score.

DO . . .
PAY YOUR BILLS IN FULL EACH MONTH AND ON TIME.

Paying all your bills on time, even if it is just the minimum amount due, is the single biggest factor in FICO's calculation of your credit scores. It accounts for

35% of your score. Now let me be clear: It is my strong advice that you pay every bill in full each month. But I want you to understand that as far as FICO is concerned, paying just the minimum due each month is good enough. As long as you get the minimum in and *on time,* your "payment history" will be strong.

DO ...
USE ONLY A SMALL PERCENTAGE
OF YOUR AVAILABLE CREDIT.

Aim to keep your combined balances on your credit cards to no more than 30% or so of your total credit limit. For example if you have three credit cards with balances of $1,000, $500, and $600 your total combined balance is $2,100. Now let's say that the three cards have credit limits of $3,000, $1,000 and $1,500. So your combined credit limit is $5,500. That means your $2,100 in outstanding balances is 38% of your total credit limit ($2,100/$5,500). There is no magic cutoff for what constitutes a good debt-to-credit-limit ratio, but the lower the better. Make it a goal to stay below 30% or so, and you should do fine on the "Amounts Owed" part of the FICO score calculation.

DON'T . . .

BE IN A RUSH TO CANCEL YOUR CREDIT CARDS.

The "length" of your credit history accounts for 15% of your FICO credit score. If you were to cancel a card with a long history, that could be a ding to your credit score. That said, it makes little sense to keep a card that charges a high annual fee. If you have other cards with established histories, it can be okay to cancel one card. Just don't cancel a bunch all at once.

The other issue with canceling a card is that it will change your total credit limit, and that will impact your debt-to-credit-limit score. For example, if you cancel a card with a $5,000 credit limit, your total credit limit will also be reduced $5,000. That will likely cause your debt-to-credit-limit ratio to rise. (See the previous item.)

DON'T . . .

OPEN LOTS OF NEW ACCOUNTS IN A SHORT PERIOD.

"New accounts" count for 10% of your FICO score. If you open more than one new account in say a period of a few months it may be a ding on your FICO score. From the lender's perspective, this can be a yellow warning sign that you are likely to increase your spending.

DON'T . . .
TAKE OUT A STORE CREDIT CARD.

Yes, I know all about the deals that are offered when you are standing in the checkout line: just sign up for the store's credit card and you'll get 10% off your purchase. Or the promise of getting 2% or 5% back if you use the card to make future purchases. Here's what I also know: cards offered by stores and department stores often charge the highest interest rates on unpaid balances. It can be more than 20%. That's crazy. If you aren't 100% confident you will always—and I mean *always*—pay off your store cards in full each month, you are to turn down any offer of a store card. This is a very important "stand in your truth" moment. I have worked with thousands of people struggling with debt who have large unpaid store-card balances charging those insane interest rates. They never thought they would let this happen, but it did. My advice: steer clear of store credit cards.

DON'T . . .

CO-SIGN A CREDIT CARD APPLICATION FOR SOMEONE ELSE.

If someone needs you to be their co-signer for a credit card, you need to realize that you and your FICO credit score are now at risk. If that person falls behind in payments, you can be held responsible for paying. And as a co-signer, the record of how that card is handled—are payments timely, is the balance high?—will impact your FICO credit score as well.

I also want you to ask yourself: Why does this person need your help? If it is an adult child who is just beginning to build credit, that's one thing. But if it is someone who has had years to build credit, but needs your help, consider that a big yellow warning signal. The credit card issuer is basically saying, "Whoa, we're concerned about this person's financial responsibility, so we are going to make sure someone else is on the hook for payments." If the card issuer is concerned, you should be concerned as well. Be careful.

If you want to help out someone by co-signing, please insist on two conditions: they are to send you the money each month, and you are to pay the bill; and you are to automatically be sent a copy of all statements so you can make sure you are aware of everything that is going on with this account.

PART 4

MANAGE SPENDING

DO ...

LIVE BELOW YOUR MEANS
BUT WITHIN YOUR NEEDS.

If you spend every dollar you have today, that leaves you nothing to put toward your savings goals: the emergency savings fund, retirement, a down payment for a home or a car. One of the biggest favors you can ever do for yourself is to shift your perspective on how you spend money. Focus your purchases on meeting your needs, but not exceeding those needs. For example, just because a $25,000 car is on sale for $22,000 does not make it a great deal. If you could meet your needs with a solid used card that costs you $18,000, you have spent $4,000 less. That's $4,000 to put toward your other goals. By living below your means, you will give yourself the biggest payoff of all: the means to build lasting financial security.

DO . . .
BE CLEAR ABOUT
WANTS VS. NEEDS.

Keeping the electricity on is a need. Gas for the car to get to work is definitely a need. The money you spend on meals out and entertainment is a want, as is money spent on gifts.

If you are finding it hard to make ends meet each month, I want you to go to suzeorman.com and use my free Expense Tracker tool to create a complete list of all your expenses. Print out a copy of your report. Now you are ready for my Needs vs. Wants challenge: I want you to circle every expense that is a want, not a need. This is yet another "stand in your truth" moment. Please be honest here. Next I want you to go through all the needs and ask yourself this important question: Can you spend even less on needs? When I work with people who tell me they can't afford to save a penny for their future, I can always—and I mean always—find wants that can be cut, but just as importantly, needs that can be trimmed as well. For example, changing your cell phone plan to the less expensive tier might save you $10 to $20 a month. Your cable/internet bill is another spot ripe for reduction. I am not telling you that you must go without, but rather, scale back your spending.

Another crucial step is to stop before you make any purchase—in a store or online—and ask yourself: Is this a want or a need? If it is a want, and you are not on track with reaching your financial goals, you and I both know the smart choice is to not make the purchase. If it is a need, just do your very best to spend the absolute least amount necessary.

DO . . .
LOOK FOR WAYS TO TRIM YOUR SPENDING.

I get how overwhelming it can be when you realize your spending is $100 or $200 or $300 or more each month than your take-home pay. I hear so many of you become instantly frustrated, *"There's nothing I can cut by $200 to close the gap."* You're probably right. There may not be one single expense you can slash by such a large amount that it will solve your income/outgo problem. But that's the wrong way to approach this challenge. Rather than focusing on finding one big expense you can slash or eliminate, how about looking for five or six or even ten expenses you can trim a little bit. When I review a family's Expense Tracker spreadsheet, they are always amazed that by cutting a little here and there the total savings can be at least a few hundred dollars a month.

DO ...
USE CASH AND DEBIT CARDS.

"Pay as you go" is the way to go as far as I am concerned. You can't get into debt if you only spend the cash you have. Walking around with a lot of cash can be impractical. A debit card that is tied to a checking account that you only keep a small amount of money in, or a prepaid debit card, is a great way to restrict your spending to what you can truly afford. An important caveat: as mentioned earlier in this section, I also recommend you have a credit card that you use a few times a month (and pay the bill in full) to help you build a strong credit score.

DON'T ...
SIGN UP FOR OVERDRAFT PROTECTION ON YOUR DEBIT CARD.

If your debit card provides overdraft protection, I want you to cancel that feature right now. If you are getting a new debit card, automatically turn down this feature. The overdraft protection completely undermines the whole point of a debit card: to spend only what you can afford. If you don't have enough money on your prepaid debit card, or enough in the checking account your debit card is linked to, isn't that the definition of unaffordable?! Besides, if you have overdraft coverage and it is used to cover a payment, you will also be hit with an overdraft fee. You're paying to spend money you don't have. Please don't make this mistake.

DON'T . . .
LINK YOUR DEBIT CARD
TO AN ACCOUNT WHERE YOU HAVE
ALL YOUR SAVINGS ON DEPOSIT.

If someone steals your debit card info, they can access your money and clean you out. While the bank may eventually refund the money if you can prove the fraud, that can take time to sort out; meanwhile you could be without your money for weeks.

Only use a debit card that is attached to an account with small amounts of money in it. Keep the rest of your money safe and sound in a different account. Or better yet use a prepaid debit card that is not attached to any of your savings.

Borrow Wise

PART 1

CAR LOANS

DO ...
TAKE OUT A CAR LOAN RATHER THAN LEASE.

If you don't have the cash to pay for a car in full you have two options: an auto loan or a lease. A loan is the far better financial move. Once the loan is paid off you will still have years ahead of you when you can continue to drive that car without owing a monthly payment. When you lease you are basically renting the car for a set period—typically 36 months. When that lease term is up you either have to buy out the lease or, as most people do, take out a new lease. That means you are always making a monthly payment. Taking out a new lease every three years is a costly financial mistake. Don't do it.

DO . . .
BUY THE LEAST EXPENSIVE CAR
THAT MEETS YOUR NEEDS.

A car is a depreciating asset. That means from the moment you drive it off the dealer's lot it is losing value. The value of a new car might fall 15% to 20% or so in just the first year you own it. So let me ask you something: If you know that you will never be able to sell or trade in your car for anywhere near what you paid for it, why would you want to spend more on that car in the first place? The best car for you is the one that meets your needs but costs the least amount of money possible. What you save in opting for the least expensive (safe) car over a more expensive model can be used to build your net worth through investments that have the potential to rise in value over time.

DO . . .
CONSIDER A USED CAR.

Before you set your sights and your heart on a brand-new car, shop the used-car lots. Especially look for a dealer who is offering cars that are just a few years old and that come with a certified pre-owned (CPO) warranty. A car that is just a few years old will cost a lot less than a new car, but given the reliability of cars manufactured today it likely has at least five to seven more good years ahead of it. With a CPO warranty you can also rest easy that key defects or issues will be covered. The best CPO warranty is a manufacturer CPO warranty. That means your car will be covered at any dealership that services cars from that manufacturer. That's smarter than a dealer CPO warranty that requires you to go to that specific dealer for future service. That can be a big drag if you happen to move far from that dealer.

DO ...

CHECK YOUR FICO CREDIT SCORE 2–3 MONTHS BEFORE YOU GO CAR SHOPPING.

Your FICO credit score is a major factor in determining the interest rate you will be offered on your car loan. In early 2014 someone with a FICO score above 720 might be able to qualify for a 36-month loan charging less than 3.4%. With a FICO credit score of 690–719, the interest rate would be 4.8%. The interest rate for someone with a FICO score between 660–689 would be 7%. Seven percent is more than double the interest charged if you have a great FICO score. That's why it is important to check your score a few months before you start car shopping. If you discover your score is below 720, I would recommend delaying your purchase until you have managed to raise your score. Curtailing your credit card spending in the months prior to a big purchase can help boost your score by reducing your debt-to-credit-limit limit ratio. (See Build a Strong Credit Score for more tips.)

DO . . .
FACTOR IN YOUR INSURANCE COSTS.

Before you settle on a specific make and model, call up your auto insurance agent or use an online auto-insurance quote site to get a sense of how much insurance will cost you for that car. Certainly the more expensive the car, the more you will pay to insure it. But there are some less obvious costs to consider as well. Cars that are popular among car thieves will often come with a higher annual insurance premium. Cars with larger engines will also typically carry a higher premium than the same make with lower horsepower.

DO . . .
LIMIT YOUR LOAN TERM TO 36 MONTHS.

Because your car is a depreciating asset you should make it your goal to borrow a sum that you can afford to pay back in 36 months. No longer than that, do you hear me? If you run the numbers and can't see how you will be able to afford the payments over 36 months, that should be a wakeup call. It means you need to shop for a less expensive car. The worst move is to fall for the trap of extending the loan to five or more years to make the monthly payment more "affordable." Please don't do it.

DO . . .
SHOP AROUND FOR THE BEST LOAN DEAL.

It may be convenient to go with the auto company's loan offer but that doesn't necessarily mean it is the best deal. Be sure to check out credit unions; they often offer the best car loan terms.

DON'T . . .
FALL FOR A 60-MONTH LOAN TERM.

The most common auto loan these days is for 60 months. That's the sneaky way the auto industry and lenders have come up with to help you "afford" a more expensive car. For example, a $25,000 car loan with a 4%

rate over a 60-month loan period would cost about $460 a month. That sounds so much better than the $738 a month it would cost if you opted for the 36-month loan rate. But c'mon, you know there's a cost to that longer loan term, right? In this example you would end up paying an extra $1,000 or so in interest payments. Besides, when you choose the 36-month loan that means at month 37 you no longer have a car payment to make. That frees up a few hundred dollars each month you can now use for other financial goals. If you took out a 60-month loan you've got another two years before you can start redirecting money to those other important goals.

It is so much smarter to lower the cost of the car you will buy so you can afford to pay it off in 36 months. If that means opting for a $20,000 loan or an $18,000 loan rather than a $25,000 loan, so be it! Remember, this is a loan for an asset that is going to lose value. Spending the least amount possible should be your goal.

DON'T . . .

LEASE. THIS BEARS REPEATING: I REALLY, REALLY, REALLY DO NOT LIKE CAR LEASES.

It puts you on a payment treadmill you will find it hard, if not impossible, to get out of.

PART 2

COLLEGE LOANS

DO . . .

FOCUS ON THE BEST AFFORDABLE COLLEGE.

I know there is much talk these days about whether college is worth it for everyone. I think that misses the point. College is indeed worth it—there are all sorts of studies showing that the lifetime earnings and opportunities for college graduates exceeds the earnings for high school graduates. But what we should be focusing on is cost. College is worth it when it is affordable. The best school is the school that works for your family's finances. I recommend that every family consider at least one "financial safety" school. That can be a public university where in-state costs are typically much lower than private-school costs, or a private school where your student will be so appealing to the college that they offer a generous aid package.

DO ...
HAVE THE STUDENT BORROW FIRST.

Your child should always borrow before you, for the simple fact that all students are eligible for federal Stafford loans, which are fixed-rate loans that charge an interest rate that is far less than other college loans. I also think it is important for children to have some "skin in the game." You may ultimately decide to help your child repay their loans, but knowing they are responsible for the Stafford loan can help them stay focused on getting the most out of their time at school.

DO ...
BORROW A SUM THAT IS LESS THAN YOUR ANTICIPATED FIRST-YEAR SALARY.

After studying the loan default rates among student borrowers, college-loan expert Mark Kantrowitz has determined that if students limit their total borrowing to less than they expect to make in their first year of work, they should be able to handle their repayments. It's when student borrow far more than their first-year salary that the incidence of defaults rises. (For the record: even if you file for bankruptcy, student loan debt is not forgiven. That's why it is so important to avoid default; even bankruptcy won't solve your problem.)

Even if your child does not have a clear career path just yet, you can still talk about how different fields—and levels of expertise—have different salary ranges. At salary.com your child can explore typical entry-level starting salaries.

DO ...
FOCUS ON FEDERAL STAFFORD LOANS.

All undergraduates are eligible for federal Stafford loans. Students whose familes qualify for financial aid may be able to get a subsidized Stafford loan. That means the government pays the interest on the loan while the student is in school. Even if you aren't eligible for financial aid, every student can get an unsubsidized Stafford loan.

The loan maximums for the 2013–14 school year are $5,500 for freshmen, $6,500 for sophomores, and $7,500 a year for juniors and seniors. In 2013 Congress voted to change the formula for setting Stafford interest rates. Beginning with the 2013–14 student year, all Stafford loans—both subsidized and unsubsidized—will have the same fixed interest rate and that rate will be reset each year based on the rate of the 10-year Treasury note.

The new Stafford interest rate formula is: the 10-year Treasury interest rate + 2.05%. In 2013–14 the fixed interest rate is 3.86%. That means a loan taken out for the 2013–14 year will have a 3.86% interest rate for the life of the loan. Once the loan is disbursed the interest rate does not change. But when you go to borrow for next year, your rate for that loan will be set based upon the prevailing 10-year Treasury rate. The maximum interest rate for a Stafford is 8.25%.

Stafford loans are your best first option because the interest rate is typically lower than other options, and that interest rate is fixed. Many private loans work like a credit card: the interest rate is variable. It may start low, but it can be adjusted higher if interest rates in general start to rise, or if penalties are levied for late payments or other problems.

One of the most important reasons to use a Stafford loan is that the federal government offers a variety of repayment programs that can take into account your income once you are out of work. You can also apply to have your payments deferred for a period if you are having trouble finding work or are ill. Private loans tend not to offer such features.

Finally, though it's unpleasant to consider, I want you to understand that if a Stafford borrower dies, the loan amount is forgiven. The surviving family will not be held responsible for the remaining balance of the loan. Private loans offer no such provision as standard policy.

At the government's Direct Loan website you can use a free calculator to get a sense of your loan repayment costs: www.direct.ed.gov/calc.html.

DO . . .

MAKE SURE YOU START REPAYMENT ON SCHEDULE.

There is typically a six-month "grace period" between when your child leaves school and when loan repayments must start. Even if your child has not landed a full-time job, they still must start repayment at that six-month mark or they must ask for forbearance or deferment before repayment is set to begin. Failure to start payments on time—or get forbearance or deferment for a period— means the loan may fall into default. And that is just plain ugly. The government can garnish the borrower's wages to get the money back. And the default will hurt the borrower's FICO credit score. Moreover, there is pretty much no way to escape student loan debt. Many debts can be forgiven in bankruptcy, but student loan debt is the one debt that is not forgiven. It stays with the borrower even if other debts have been forgiven in bankruptcy.

DO ...
DEDUCT YOUR STUDENT LOAN INTEREST.

The interest you pay on a student loan can be claimed as a federal tax deduction. In 2014 the maximum amount of student loan interest you could deduct was $2,500. Your federal modified adjusted gross income (MAGI) for 2014 must be below $65,000 ($130,000 if filing a joint return) to claim the full deduction. You can take this deduction even if you don't file an itemized return.

DO ...
TAKE OUT A TERM LIFE INSURANCE POLICY ON THE STUDENT IF YOU CO-SIGN A PRIVATE LOAN.

To be clear, my strong preference is that no one in your family use a private loan to finance college. But in the event that you end up with a private loan, you need to understand that if the student were to die, the loan balance will not be automatically forgiven. Some lenders may ultimately agree to forgive the balance, but they are not required to, and they may insist that the co-signer make good. (All federal student loans are forgiven in the event that the student/borrower dies.) So to protect yourself, take out a term life insurance policy for the amount of the total loan balance. It should be very inexpensive and is a crucial way to protect yourself if you have co-signed.

DO . . .

TRY TO REPAY YOUR FEDERAL STUDENT LOANS UNDER THE STANDARD REPAYMENT METHOD.

As mentioned earlier, there are a variety of repayment plans for federal loans. I still want you to make it your goal to see if you can sign up for the standard repayment plan that will have your loan completely paid off in 10 years. Just try it. You are going to feel so great to be rid of this debt in 10 years, rather than using a repayment plan that drags on for more years.

DO . . .

CONSIDER A PUBLIC-SERVICE JOB AS A WAY TO REDUCE YOUR STUDENT LOAN REPAYMENT.

Work full time at a qualifying public-service job, and after 10 years of on-time loan payments any remaining balance will be forgiven. (If you opt for this route, you obviously want to use a repayment plan with a longer, not shorter, repayment schedule.) You can learn more at http://studentaid.ed.gov.

DO . . .

MAKE PAYING BACK YOUR STUDENT LOAN THE VERY FIRST BILL YOU PAY.

It is more important that you make your student loan payments on time each month than any other bill. As I have mentioned, student loans are the one debt that by law cannot be wiped out in bankruptcy. And the government has all sorts of ways to get the money— including taking it out of your paycheck. Bottom line, do not fall behind in your student loans. Make paying this debt on time every month your top priority.

DON'T...

TAKE OUT A FEDERAL PLUS LOAN UNLESS YOU ARE ON TRACK WITH YOUR RETIREMENT SAVINGS.

Parents can take out a Federal PLUS loan to help pay for a child's undergraduate years. Like a Stafford loan the interest rate on a PLUS is fixed. The formula for the PLUS loan is the interest rate on a 10-year Treasury note +4.6%. For the 2013–14 year the rate is 6.41%. Once the loan is disbursed the interest rate does not change. But when you go to borrow for next year, your rate for that loan will be set based upon the prevailing 10-year Treasury rate. The maximum interest rate that may be charged in subsequent years is 10.25%.

At 6.25% a fixed-rate PLUS loan is still a better deal than a variable-rate private loan. But here's the deal, parents: you should not borrow a penny for a child's college education if you are not on track with your retirement savings. Think that sounds harsh? It's anything but. Putting your retirement ahead of your child's college costs is the most loving decision. I want you to be financially secure in your retirement so you don't have to turn to your adult children for help. There are loans for college your child can take out. There are not loans for you to be able to live comfortably in retirement.

If you do decide to take out a PLUS loan, please borrow a responsible amount that you are confident you will have repaid before you retire. One of the problems with PLUS loans is that there is no effective loan limit; you can borrow as much as is needed to cover the bill after factoring in all financial aid. Just because you may be allowed to borrow a large sum does not mean you should. At the government's Direct Loan website you can use a free calculator to get a sense of your loan repayment costs: www.direct.ed.gov/calc.html.

DON'T ...
FALL FOR A PRIVATE STUDENT LOAN.

Most private student loans have variable interest rates. That means that as general interest rates rise, the interest on a private student loan will also rise. And there's a good chance rates will rise in the coming years. As I write this in early 2014, interest rates are near historic lows as the Federal Reserve continues to use low interest rates as a tool to help the economy continue its recovery from the financial crisis that began in 2008. Today's interest rates are not "normal." So if you were to take out a private student loan today with an adjustable rate, that means you better be prepared to pay a higher rate in the future. I also don't like the fact that private loans typically don't offer the same lenient repayment options that you can get with federal loans.

DON'T . . .
FALL BEHIND IN YOUR PAYMENTS.

This bears repeating: if you don't make your student loan payments on time, your account will be considered to be in default. A loan that is in default will have a negative impact on your FICO credit score. It can also mean that your wages will be "garnished"—the government has the right to take money out of your paycheck before you are even paid. It can also grab your federal tax refund and put it toward your student loan bill. And I am going to spell this out again, it is so very important: Student loan debt is not forgiven when you apply for bankruptcy; you will still owe the money.

DON'T ...
USE A HOME EQUITY LOAN
OR HOME EQUITY LINE OF CREDIT
TO PAY FOR COLLEGE.

This is for parents: please do not tap your home's equity to cover college costs. Your home is the collateral for both types of loans. If you fall behind on your home equity loan (HEL) or home equity line of credit (HELOC) payments, you could lose your home to foreclosure. I know you want to help your children, but putting your home at risk is not a solution.

DON'T ...
STOP OR CURTAIL RETIREMENT SAVINGS
TO PAY FOR A CHILD'S COLLEGE.

Every parent's number one priority is to do their very best to make sure they will be able to support themselves through their retirement. As I have said before and I will keep saying until it sinks in: There are loans for your child's college education. There are no loans for retirement. Think about this for a moment: If you scale back your retirement savings to pay for college costs, it raises the odds that you will need to turn to your children when they

THE DO'S AND DON'TS OF MONEY

are adults—and probably in the midst of raising their own kids—for financial assistance. That's going to be a hard burden for them. I know from adult children who are in this very predicament today that they wish their parents had been upfront with them about the situation when they were heading to college. They all say they would have attended a less expensive school or worked part time to cover the costs if they had understood how their parents were making a costly tradeoff by not keeping up with their retirement savings.

DON'T . . .

MAKE THE INCOME-BASED REPAYMENT (IBR) METHOD YOUR FIRST CHOICE.

It can be very tempting to sign up for the IBR plan (if you qualify) as it will typically result in much lower payments than you will have if you use the standard 10-year repayment plan. And as you may have heard, if you keep making payments under IBR for 25 years, any remaining balance will then be forgiven. But there's a catch with that: the amount that is forgiven may be reported to the IRS as income, and you would need to pay tax on it. Just something to be aware of. Besides, as

I mentioned earlier, it would be so great to be rid of this debt in 10 years (with no tax bill) rather than have to deal with it for 25 years.

PART 3

MISCELLANEOUS LOAN ADVICE

DON'T . . .

TAKE OUT A CREDIT-CARD CASH ADVANCE.

This is hands-down one of the most expensive ways to borrow money. The interest charged on a cash advance starts the day you take out the money. There is no grace period. Even if you pay it all back when your next credit card bill is due, you will have still paid interest. And the average annual interest rate is 22%. There will also be a fee for taking out the cash advance. The minimum fee is $10 and the maximum is typically 3% to 5% of the loan amount. If you follow my advice and begin to create an emergency fund that will eventually cover up to eight months of your living costs, you should never have the need to take out a costly credit-card cash advance.

DON'T ...

TAKE OUT A PAYDAY LOAN.

A 2012 study by the Pew Charitable Trusts found that the average payday loan is $375 and the borrower will typically end up paying $520 over just five months on the initial $375. As bad as a cash advance is, a payday loan is just a horrible, horrible deal. Again, the faster you can commit to building an emergency savings account, the lower the odds will be that you will ever consider a payday loan.

DON'T ...

TAKE A LOAN FROM YOUR 401(K).
THIS IS A BAD DEAL FOR A FEW REASONS.

Your account balance will be reduced by the amount of the loan; if the markets rise during the time of your loan, you have less money that is growing. You must repay the loan—typically within five years—and that money will come from your after—tax income. Then when you retire and withdraw the money, you will owe tax on the withdrawal. So you've paid tax twice on the money you used to repay your loan. A common strategy when repaying the loan is to reduce the amount you are contributing to the account; that's just doubling up on your problem: you want to be putting more money into the account to make up for the time when you reduced the balance—not less! And finally, it is important to understand that if you were to leave your job—voluntarily or not—you typically must repay the loan within 90 days or so. If you fail to meet the deadline, the loan will be considered a withdrawal. If you are under 55 years old you will owe a 10% early withdrawal penalty on the balance of the loan/withdrawal, and all money withdrawn from a traditional 401(k) is always taxed as ordinary income. (See Section 4, Retirement Planning, for more on 401(k) Do's and Don'ts.)

DON'T . . .

TAKE OUT A HOME EQUITY LOAN OR HOME EQUITY LINE OF CREDIT FOR A WANT.

A home equity loan (HEL) is a fixed-rate loan that gives you a lump sum of money to use as you wish. A home equity line of credit (HELOC) is typically a variable-rate line that you can draw on whenever you want. Both loans use your home as collateral. If you were to fall behind on your HEL or HELOC payments you could be forced to sell the home. That makes it foolish to use either type of loan to finance a want unless you have other savings or assets you know you could tap to cover the payments.

Moreover, I would be very careful using a HELOC at this time. As I write this in early 2014, interest rates are still well below their historic norms because of Federal Reserve policy decisions. We don't know exactly when interest rates will begin to rise—but it is a question of when, not it. And when that happens, the interest rate charged on HELOCs will rise as well.

DON'T . . .
CO-SIGN A LOAN UNLESS YOU CAN AFFORD TO PAY FOR THE ENTIRE LOAN.

This should be abundantly clear: when you co-sign a loan you are telling the lender (and FICO) that you agree to make good on the repayment if the borrower slips up. I don't care how responsible and conscientious someone may be; they may be hit with one of life's costly and unpredictable "what ifs." And if that happens, you will be on the hook to make the payments on any loan you co-sign. It's really simple: If you couldn't afford to repay the loan in full, you should never agree to co-sign in the first place.

DON'T . . .

ASK A FAMILY OR A FRIEND FOR A LOAN IF YOU KNOW IT WILL UNDERMINE THEIR FINANCIAL SECURITY.

There is no more ungracious act than to knowingly ask someone for money if you have even a slight inkling they can't truly afford to help. You should be very direct: If you ask them for a loan, make it clear that you will only accept their help if they will still have at least eight months of savings set aside in their emergency fund. If they don't yet have eight months of savings, or loaning you money will reduce their emergency fund below that level, the responsible and loving act is to not accept the loan.

If someone can afford to loan you money, you are to formalize the deal by creating and signing a simple promissory installment note to show them you are serious about this transaction. You can download a free promissory note template at suzeorman.com.

Part of showing your respect is to pay the loan back with interest. In fact, the Internal Revenue Service expects you to pay interest as well. The IRS sets a minimum interest rate for loans, called the Applicable Federal Rate (AFR). In early 2014 the AFR for a loan term of less than three years was 0.25% and 1.75% for a loan with a term of between three and nine years.

Your Home

HOME BUYING

DO ...

UNDERSTAND THE TOTAL COST OF HOME OWNERSHIP.

If you are considering buying your first home, it's vitally important to not assume that the mortgage is your only big cost. In addition to the monthly mortgage, you will also owe property tax, and your homeowner's insurance will be more expensive than renter's insurance. You also need to factor in the cost of the upkeep of your home: You're going to be the landlord now! My advice is to plan for all those additional costs by adding 30% to your mortgage cost. So if the monthly mortgage is $1,000, add another $300. That $1,300 is a more realistic estimate of your *total* housing costs.

DO ...
PLAY HOUSE.

This is also for the first-timers: Six months before you begin to house hunt, I want you to start saving 30% of your current rent in a savings account. So if your rent is $1,000 a month, you are to have $300 a month automatically moved from a checking account into your new "Play House" account. As explained in the previous item, first-timers often underestimate the extra costs of home ownership. If you can handle the 30% in extra savings for six months then you know for sure you should be able to handle a mortgage amount that is equal to your current monthly rent.

DO ...
GET PREAPPROVED FOR A MORTGAGE.

If you are aiming to buy a house when the market is strong and there are more buyers than sellers, an important way to stand out among other buyers is to be able to show a seller that you already have been preapproved for a mortgage. (Your lender will provide a letter.) When sellers can choose from multiple offers, they will likely be most interested in a competitive offer from a buyer who already has financing lined up. (See the next Part, Mortgages, for more on this topic.)

DO ...

WORK WITH A LENDER WHO WORKS FAST.

If you are looking to buy in a market where there is competition among buyers (known as a seller's market) make sure your lender has a good reputation for getting loan deals closed promptly. Here's why: In a seller's market the seller may receive multiple offers from potential buyers. If all the offers are comparable in terms of price, the deciding factor could be whose offer comes with financing from a lender with a good reputation for fast closes. The seller's agent will be advising her client on which lenders in fact have the best reputation for getting deals done.

DO . . .

EXTRA HOMEWORK
IF YOU ARE CONSIDERING CONDOS.

If you are considering buying a condominium, you need to make sure that the finances of the condo association are in good shape. Find out how many times the monthly maintenance has been raised during the past five years, and by how much. It should not have increased more than the rate of inflation. Confirm that at least 10% of monthly maintenance costs are put aside in a reserve fund to help with big-ticket maintenance costs. Find out if there has been a special assessment (and how much) in the past five years; that happens when there is costly maintenance and not enough was set aside in the reserve fund. Confirm that at least 90% of the units are owner-occupied rather than investment properties that are rented. That's a sign you will be living with people who are just as "invested" in the property as you are. It will also make it easier to obtain a mortgage.

DO ...

MAKE SURE YOUR HOME INSURANCE IS FOR EXTENDED REPLACEMENT COST.

There are three levels of home insurance: Actual Cost Value, Replacement Cost, and Extended Replacement Cost. Never settle for Actual Cost Value. It will likely come with the lowest premium, but that's because you're only reimbursed the *depreciated* value of anything that is damaged or stolen. So for example, if your 10-year-old roof springs a major leak, your coverage will reflect the cost of it being a 10-year-old roof. You want your policy to cover the full cost of replacing it with new materials. That's what Replacement Cost gets you. Even better is Extended Replacement Cost coverage, where the payout can be as much as 125% of your stated policy coverage. That's important coverage in the event that you have a major loss; if you need to rebuild or do major repairs, you may find that your policy's limit hasn't kept up with the recent building costs. (That's another Do: review your policy every year!)

DON'T . . .

BUY A HOUSE IF YOU PLAN
TO MOVE WITHIN FIVE YEARS.

The cost of paying the agent's fee—typically 6% or so—sprucing up your house, settling any transfer taxes with your state or county, and the cost of moving can easily add up to 10% or so of your sale price. That's why I don't recommend buying a home if you intend to live in it for just a few years. You might need at least 10% appreciation in the home's value just to cover the cost of selling. While over long stretches home values have kept pace with inflation, we have no guarantee what will ever happen over short periods. The last thing you want is to be ready to move on with your life and end up selling at a net loss after factoring in all the costs.

DON'T . . .

BASE YOUR PURCHASE PRICE ON THE TAX
SAVINGS.

If you file a federal tax return where you itemize your deductions, you are allowed to deduct the interest payments on your mortgage. That can indeed be a big deal in the early years of the mortgage, when most of your payment is interest, not principal. But I never want you to factor in the tax savings when you are deciding how big a mortgage you can afford. It's far smarter and safer to base your mortgage budget on your income, plain and simple. Consider the mortgage-interest deduction as a "bonus." This will keep you from stretching too far on the size of your mortgage.

DON'T . . .

BUY WITHOUT A
PROFESSIONAL HOME INSPECTION.

We all know that housing markets tend to go to extremes: they can be very hot or very cold. And when they are very hot, people feel pressured (sometimes by their agents) to make an offer that waives the home inspection. That's a very bad strategy. You are about to spend $150,000, $200,000, or maybe $2 million on a home, and you're telling me you don't care if there are serious problems? If the reality of the market is that a bid with a home-inspection contingency won't be considered by sellers, you have two options. Wait for the market to cool down. It always does. Or, if you are very very serious about this home, ask to conduct a home inspection prior to when bids will be taken. The risk here is that the $400 or so you might spend on the home inspection could be lost if your bid isn't the winning bid. Still, I'd rather be out that $400 than buy a home that needs tens of thousands of dollars of repairs.

DON'T ...

SETTLE FOR ACTUAL COST VALUE FOR YOUR HOME INSURANCE.

As I explained earlier in this section, Actual Cost Value will only pay you the depreciated value of replacing and repairing covered losses.

PART 2

MORTGAGES

DO . . .

CHOOSE A FIXED-RATE MORTGAGE.

A fixed-rate mortgage means the interest rate that determines your payment will never change. When you're mortgage shopping, you will see offers for adjustable-rate mortgages that—at first glance—look like a better deal because the rate is in fact lower than on a fixed-rate mortgage. But as its name implies, adjustable means the rate can change; it will move up and down based on a widely followed benchmark index, such as the LIBOR interest rate. As I write this in early 2014, interest rates remain near their historic lows. Nobody knows exactly when they will start to rise. But it is a question of when, not if. That's why I recommend sticking with a fixed-rate mortgage. Today's sub-5% rate for borrowers with a strong FICO credit score is still amazingly great!

DO ...

CONSIDER A 15-YEAR MORTGAGE.

If you are in your 40s or 50s and looking to buy a home, I want you to think about an important financial goal: being able to retire with your mortgage paid off. That will remove a major "expense" when you are living on a fixed income. A 15-year mortgage obviously means your monthly mortgage payment will be higher than if you are spreading the payments out over 30 years. But it means you can retire mortgage-free. And because interest rates are still very low (as of early 2014), a 15-year loan is more affordable than it has been in more than 10 years. I encourage you to run the numbers (at my website suzeorman.com I have a free Mortgage Calculator) to get a sense of what your payments might be with a 15-year mortgage. Keep in mind, one way to lower the cost is to lower your housing budget. A less expensive home that you can finance with a 15-year loan can be a great retirement planning move.

DO ...

TRY TO MAKE A DOWN PAYMENT OF AT LEAST 20%.

Yes, I know FHA-insured mortgages require a down payment of as little as 3.5%. But I think it is smart to make a 20% down payment. When you make a 20% down payment, you will not be required to purchase additional private mortgage insurance (PMI). Anything less than 20% and you've got PMI to deal with. The other reason I like a higher down payment is that it is a signal you are truly prepared and ready to take on the responsibility of home ownership. If you need a few years to save up a sizable down payment, that's smarter in my book than rushing into a low-down-payment loan that charges you PMI. (And to be clear: on an FHA-insured loan you will indeed be paying an extra insurance premium; and even once your equity in the home rises above 20%, you will still be required to keep paying the insurance premium on your FHA loan.)

DO ...
SET UP AUTO PAY FOR YOUR MORTGAGE PAYMENT.

Right when you sign the papers to take out your mortgage, I want you also to sign up to have your monthly payment automatically sent from your checking account. This is too big and too important a bill to ever trip up on. You sure don't want late mortgage payments to show up in your credit reports; that would hurt your FICO credit score. Set the transfer date at least three business days before the due date.

DO ...
AIM TO LIVE MORTGAGE-FREE IN RETIREMENT.

Not having the big monthly cost of a mortgage in retirement is going to be a major stress reducer in retirement. If you are in your 50s and living in a home you plan to retire in, accelerate your payments now to make sure you have the mortgage paid off before you retire. The Mortgage Calculator at my website, suzeorman.com, lets you see how adding one extra payment a year (or more frequently) will speed up your repayment schedule.

DO ...

PROVIDE ALL DOCUMENTATION REQUESTED BY YOUR LENDER.

Mortgage lenders are very, very careful these days when considering loan applications. You may be amazed (and dazed) by all the financial documentation you will need to provide: copies of tax returns, retirement accounts, and months of bank records to track your spending. But if you want to get the mortgage, you better step up and provide every document that is requested. If you don't provide a complete set of requested documents, chances are your loan will not be approved. It may seem like a bit of overkill to you, but that's just the rules of the game right now. Take a deep breath and remind yourself that in four to six weeks or so this will all be over and you will have the house of your dreams.

DO ...
PAY YOUR PROPERTY TAX
AND INSURANCE YOURSELF.

Some mortgage lenders want to create an escrow account that you fund and that the lender then uses to pay your insurance and property tax. (It typically shows up as an additional monthly cost added to your mortgage.) I really don't like this arrangement. I have more faith that you will make those important payments on time. If a lender mentions escrow, ask if it is mandatory.

DON'T ...
LET A LENDER TELL YOU WHAT
YOUR MORTGAGE LIMIT IS.

A mortgage lender will take your basic income and debt information and run a few quick calculations to tell you how big a mortgage you will be able to qualify for. Don't pay any attention to this. What the lender doesn't ask about—but what is a huge part of your financial security—are other important goals you have. Such as saving for retirement. Or a child's college education. Or helping out your parents. If you take out the maximum mortgage the lender approves, will you be able to fund those important goals? Listen to me here: you and only you should decide how big a mortgage you can afford, because only you have the big picture in mind.

DON'T . . .
MISTAKE PREQUALIFIED FOR PREAPPROVED.

When a mortgage lender gives you a prequalification letter, all it basically means is you look like a good candidate for a mortgage up to a certain amount. If you are house hunting during a time when there are many buyers vying for homes, I recommend you get a mortgage preapproval before you start shopping. This is a much more involved process, where the lender requests a lot of documents, checks your FICO credit score, and does a thorough analysis to determine if you are qualified for a mortgage—and if so, how large. In markets where there is a lot of competition among buyers, you want your offer to include a preapproved letter. It signals to the seller that you will be able to close the deal. No seller wants to accept a bid and then find out in a week or two that the buyer's mortgage deal fell through. To get your bid considered, get a mortgage preapproval.

DON'T . . .
SIGN UP FOR A PREPAYMENT PLAN.

The bank or financial institution that handles your mortgage may offer you a special program that will help you pay off your mortgage faster. For a fee of course. Don't fall for it. You can do this for free: just send in extra payments when you want. (Tip: make sure your extra payments are applied only to principal—not interest.) At my website, suzeorman.com, the free Mortgage Calculator will show you how prepayments will speed up your repayment time frame.

DON'T . . .
TAKE OUT A HOME EQUITY LOAN OR HOME EQUITY LINE OF CREDIT FOR WANTS.

A home equity loan (HEL) is typically a fixed-rate loan that pays you a lump sum to use as you please. A home equity line of credit (HELOC) is typically a variable-rate loan that gives you a line of credit you can draw against when needed. First things first: neither is ever to be used for a want. Your home is the collateral for this loan. That means if something happens and you can't repay, you could lose your home. Now if you have a legitimate need, I prefer a HEL over a HELOC. Yes, a HEL typically has a higher interest rate these days, but remember that rate is fixed. It will never change. The interest rate on a HELOC will rise when general rates rise. Right now interest rates are still near historic lows. At some point we will see rates rise. If you've got a big HELOC balance, your payments will rise as well. That's just too risky. The only scenario where a HELOC is okay is if you are 100% sure you will repay the line within 12 months or so. Tip: Credit unions often have the best HEL and HELOC rates.

DON'T ...
EXTEND YOUR MORTGAGE LENGTH WHEN YOU REFINANCE.

If you refinance a mortgage, you should always aim to have your new mortgage match the remaining time on your old mortgage. For instance, let's say you started with a 30-year mortgage that you've been paying off for 10 years. So you have 20 years left. If you want to refinance, you should ask for 15- or 20-year mortgage. What you want to avoid is refinancing into another 30-year mortgage and using the entire 30 years to repay the loan. That means your total mortgage term would be 40 years (10 years on the first loan and 30 years on the refinanced loan). Taking 40 years to repay the loan rather than a total of 30 years means thousands of dollars more in interest payments.

PART 3

SELLING A HOME

DO ...

HIRE AN AGENT WITH EXPERTISE IN YOUR NEIGHBORHOOD AND PRICE POINT.

You would never go see a heart surgeon for a bad knee, right? When it comes to selling your home, you want to work with a real estate agent who truly specializes in the characteristics of your home. Everyone has a niche. Some agents are known for selling high-end trade-up homes while others are focused on neighborhoods with more affordable homes. Some agents are dialed into the condo market, others aren't. Work with an agent who truly knows how to get the most value for your home.

DO ...

BASE YOUR LIST PRICE ON CURRENT MARKET TRENDS.

Any real estate agent you are considering should base their suggested list price on a thorough market analysis that reflects current trends. This analysis should be part of every agent's pitch to you—before you sign a listing agreement. Do not accept a verbal pitch. You want to see in writing what the agent is using to determine the list price. It should reflect sales in your neighborhood—ideally your street if possible—that have occurred in the past month or two. The older the "comp" the more you need to know about the current trend in whether homes are selling faster or slower, and whether the sale price is trending higher or lower relative to the list price. That gives you an important sense of momentum in your market.

DO ...

FACTOR IN THE TOTAL COST OF SELLING.

The single biggest expense when you sell is likely the sales commission you will owe. Sellers pay 100% of the commission, which is typically 6%. But there can be many other expenses, such as state and local transfer taxes, staging expenses, sprucing up the home (paint, cleaning up the yard), and hiring the movers, that can push the total cost of selling to 10% or so of the final sale price. Factor in your potential net profit (or loss) before you list. It can help you decide whether you want to sell right now, or how big a down payment you may be able to make on your next home.

DO ...

CONSIDER A HOME INSPECTION PRIOR TO LISTING.

This can become an important tool in your sales strategy. You have two choices: you can address any issues raised in the home inspection prior to listing the home, or you can list "as is" with your sales price accounting for the expected cost of any recommended repairs. The value is that there are no surprises for the buyer (who will still likely have another inspection done). That reduces the chances you'll accept a bid from a buyer who then gets cold feet after a home inspection and pulls her offer. That costs you precious time, and studies show the longer a home stays on the market, the lower the final sale price.

DO . . .

CONSIDER OFFERING A HOME WARRANTY.

If your home is likely to attract first-time home buyers, consider purchasing a one-year home warranty that covers mechanical glitches, such as a dishwasher that goes on the fritz. It can help allay the concerns of cash-strapped first-timers. The cost is typically $300 to $500 or so.

DO . . .

BE PRESENT FOR THE HOME APPRAISAL.

If your buyer is going to use a mortgage to make the purchase, a home appraisal will be required. It is in your best interests to have the house appraise for at least as much as the agreed upon sale price. Ever since the financial crisis, appraisals have increasingly been a sticking point in some deals, as the appraisal comes in below the offering price. That triggers a whole new round of negotiations. The seller might have to reduce the sale price, or the buyer has to come up with a bigger down payment, or the deal falls apart and you're back at square one.

One way to increase the odds an appraiser will correctly value your house is to be present for the walk-through so you can answer questions and politely explain the upgrades and repairs you've made. If there has been extensive work done, prepare a spreadsheet for the appraiser, listing all your projects and the scope of the work.

DON'T . . .

BASE THE LIST PRICE ON WHAT YOU PAID FOR THE HOUSE.

What you paid for your home is irrelevant in terms of setting your asking price when you go to sell. Yes, I absolutely understand that your purchase price is very relevant to you. But the fact that you paid $250,000 for your home eight years ago and want to walk away "whole" doesn't matter if the current market value based on recent comparable sales puts the value at $230,000. If you want to sell, you must understand current market realities.

DON'T . . .
SKIMP ON LOW-COST PRIMPING.

Painting the interior might cost you $1,000 or so (if you hire pros). Renting a storage unit so you can do some serious de-cluttering can run $150 or so a month. Real estate agents will tell you from experience that those costs will be more than recouped as buyers gravitate toward clean spaces.

DON'T . . .
ASSUME YOU MUST PAY
A 6% SALES COMMISSION.

Agents deserve to be paid for their services, but the standard 6% sales commission is not some set-in-stone law. It is in fact negotiable. In 2012 the national average was in fact 5.4%. (For the record: the 6% is split between the firms representing the buyer and the seller.) As counter-intuitive as it may sound, in a soft or slow market where homes don't sell quickly, you should lean toward a higher commission as it is likely going to take some time and serious marketing effort to land a buyer who makes a solid offer. In a seller's market—where there aren't enough homes to meet buyer demand—you may be able to negotiate a lower commission. Agents in seller's markets are hungry for listings, and they also know they will likely not need to spend as much time or money marketing the property. That can give them more incentive to accept a slightly lower commission rate.

Retirement Planning

THE BIG PICTURE

DO ...

UNDERSTAND LONGEVITY.

A 65-year-old woman today has a life expectancy of 85. For a 65-year-old man, the average life expectancy is age 83. Now here's what I really want you to get: that doesn't mean you should plan on dying at age 85/83. A life expectancy of age 85 means that half of today's 65-year-old women will die before age 85 and half will still be alive at age 85. That's the important point here: there's a 50% chance of still being alive at age 85 and beyond. If you are currently in good health, and your family has a history of living into their 80s and beyond, your retirement planning should be focused on making sure you will be financially secure until age 90 or 95. That's how you address longevity risk.

DO ...

CONSIDER WORKING
UNTIL AT LEAST AGE 65.

If you retire at age 60 (or sooner) you could be facing 30 years or more where you are living off of retirement income. For most of us, asking our retirement savings to support us for nearly as long as our working days is asking a lot. If you anticipate that Social Security will be a major piece of your retirement income, working longer is especially smart. As I will explain, delaying when you start to take your Social Security retirement benefit will entitle you to a much bigger benefit.

DO ...

ANTICIPATE OUT-OF-POCKET
HEALTH CARE EXPENSES IN RETIREMENT.

When you reach age 65 you will be able to enroll in Medicare, which will cover most of your health care costs. But not all. There is the monthly premium you pay for Medicare coverage, as well as deductibles, co-payments, and the cost of any treatments not covered by Medicare.

By some estimates, a 65-year-old couple in 2014 should plan on needing more than $200,000 to cover health care expenses through their retirement that will not be covered by Medicare. I know that sounds like a lot—it is a lot!—but remember part of the equation is the fact that at least one spouse could live into his or her 90s.

DO . . .
FACTOR IN THE BITE OF INFLATION.

Given the prospect of a very long life, it is very important to focus on how inflation plays into your retirement plan. Inflation measures the rise in prices. (Deflation, falling prices, is very rare, as if I need to point that out!) If inflation averages a moderate 3% a year, it will reduce the purchasing power of $1 today to less than 50 cents in 25 years. Or let's flip that around: What you pay $1 for today you will need more than $2 to pay for in 25 years. What's that got to do with retirement planning? As we will explain, you want your investment portfolio to gain more over time than inflation. Otherwise, how will you pay for your living costs in retirement? And over time—I am talking decades—stocks have produced the best inflation-beating returns.

DO . . .

START SAVING FOR RETIREMENT ASAP.

Time is the biggest friend you will have when it comes to building retirement security. The earlier you begin to save, the less money you will need to invest to meet your goals. All because of the magic of compound growth. Someone who starts saving $200 a month at age 25 and keeps it up for 40 years will have nearly $400,000 at age 65 assuming a 6% annualized rate of return. Wait until age 30 to start saving, and at age 65, there will be just $285,000 in the retirement account. Wait until age 45 to start saving $200 a month, and there will be only less than $100,000 saved up by age 65.

For the late starter to end up with $400,000 by age 65, it would take a monthly investment of around $850 beginning at age 45. That's a tall order! It is natural to think you have plenty of time to get serious about saving for retirement. And let's be honest, it's not the easiest thing to push ourselves to save today for a goal that can be decades away. I get it. But please hear me: the sooner you start, the easier you will find it to build the security you want and need for your retirement years.

DON'T ...

TOUCH YOUR RETIREMENT SAVINGS UNLESS YOU HAVE A SERIOUS EMERGENCY.

Spending your retirement money before you retire is a serious mistake. Yes, I know all about taking loans from your 401(k)—with the intention of paying yourself back. But that is still not a good deal. For starters, there's the possibility you may not get it all repaid. If that happens it will be considered a *withdrawal* and you will then owe income tax on the loan amount (that is now counted as a withdrawal) and a 10% early withdrawal penalty if you are younger than 59½. (Note: individuals who leave a job at age 55 can make withdrawals and not owe the 10% early withdrawal penalty.) More importantly, what are you going to rely on for income when you do retire? And during the time you're repaying the loan, you've reduced the money inside the account that can compound for you. There's also a second tax hit on the money you repay into your account. When you retire and take withdrawals from your traditional 401(k) account, that money will be taxed at your ordinary income tax rate. How does that make sense?

PART 2

INVESTING FOR RETIREMENT

DO ...
FOCUS ON YOUR GOAL, NOT YOUR RETIREMENT DATE.

When you decide to stop working (or working full time) is going to be a big marker in your life. It's one of the biggest transitions we experience. But it should not be the focus of your investment strategy. Your asset allocation strategy—your mix of stocks, bonds, and cash—needs to support you through your entire life. As we've just discussed, that might be 25 to 30 years past the date when you stop working full time. When it comes to investing for retirement, you want to think about making sure your money will last longer than you! And that could be into your 90s.

DO . . .
DIVERSIFY.

There are two levels of diversification you want to follow. The first is to make sure you have a smart mix of stocks, bonds, and cash. Stocks provide the opportunity for inflation-beating gains over the long-term. Bonds are less volatile than stocks, but over time they have delivered lower returns than stocks. And because we are currently in a situation where interest rates are abnormally low, we must prepare for the fact that in the coming years, bonds will likely not produce the high returns they have for the past 20 years. That's because when interest rates rise, bond prices fall. Cash is of course the "safest" investment, in that you will not lose any principal. But there's a risk in cash too: if your cash earns 1% or 2% and inflation averages 3% or 4%, the purchasing power of your cash will not keep up with prices. The right mix of stocks, bonds, and cash is a personal choice. A good rule of thumb to consider is to subtract your age from 100 (or 110 if longevity is a family trait). That number is the percentage you might consider investing in stocks. So if you are 30, you might have 70% or 80% invested in stocks. If you are 65 you might have 35% to 45% invested in stocks.

Once you decide on your stock/bond/cash mix, mutual funds and exchange traded funds (ETFs) are a smart way to add another important type of diversification. Funds and ETFs are portfolios that typically own dozens and often hundreds of different investments. That's a great way to make sure your investments aren't riding on just a handful of stocks or bonds.

DO ...
FOCUS ON LOW FEES.

One of the best ways to increase your retirement savings is to make sure the fees you pay to invest in a mutual fund or ETF are as low as possible. All funds and ETFs charge an ongoing annual fee called the expense ratio. The difference between investing in a portfolio that charges 1% a year and one that charges just 0.25% a year can add up to tens of thousands of dollars over decades of investing. There are many low-cost index mutual funds and ETFs with fees below 0.5% and plenty that charge less than 0.25%.

DON'T . . .

PUT COLLEGE SAVINGS AHEAD OF RETIREMENT SAVINGS.

I respect how much every parent (and grandparent) wants to help their children and grandchildren. But shortchanging your retirement savings so you can put money away for college is not going to help either you or your children. Please take a careful look at the long-term: If you don't have enough saved for retirement, you will likely turn to your children for help, just at a point in their adult life when they are juggling their own important financial goals, such as raising a family and saving for their own retirement. Will they help you? Of course! They are your kids. But the best gift you can give them is to avoid needing their help at all. If you get to retirement in great financial shape that will allow your adult children to focus on their financial goals, and not have to worry about you. That's why I want you to make retirement savings your number one priority. College savings is only to be done if you honestly know your retirement savings is on track. In Section 2, Borrow Wise, you and your children can read my advice for how to tackle paying for college. Remember: there are loans for college, but no loans for retirement.

DON'T . . .

INVEST IN LONG-TERM BOND FUNDS.

For more than 25 years, bond fund investors have had little to worry about. When interest rates fall—as they have since the 1980s—bond prices rise. So the total return (yield + price) has been strong. But now we face a future where today's abnormally low interest rates will rise over time. When interest rates rise, bond prices fall; that will reduce a bond fund's total return.

The longer the maturity of the bonds in a portfolio, the more sensitive it is to changing interest rates. In a rising-rate environment, funds with long-term bonds will suffer bigger losses than shorter-term bond funds. A good and quick way to measure a fund's interest rate risk is to focus on duration. (Every fund or retirement plan sponsor should have this information available on their website.) Duration tells you how a fund will react if interest rates change by 1 percentage point. A fund with a 15-year duration will have a 15% price decline if rates rise 1 percentage point. A fund with a 5-year duration will have a 5% price decline if rates rise 1 percentage point.

I know many of you invest in bond funds through your 401(k) or IRA. If so, my strong recommendation is to not invest in any fund with a duration greater than five years or so.

PART 3

401(K) AND 403(B) RETIREMENT ACCOUNTS

NOTE:
For simplicity, this section refers to 401(k) plans;
however, the advice also applies to 403(b) plans.

DO ...

MAKE THIS YOUR PRIORITY IF YOU GET A COMPANY MATCHING CONTRIBUTION.

If your employer offers a matching contribution, you must participate in the plan! Do you hear me? You wouldn't turn down a bonus, right? Well, an employer match is just like a bonus. If you agree to contribute to your account, your company will add money to that account. Always, always, always make it your first retirement saving priority to contribute enough to your retirement account so you will qualify for the maximum matching contribution from your employer.

DO . . .

MAKE SURE YOU ARE GETTING THE MAXIMUM MATCHING CONTRIBUTION.

Every employer chooses the formula for how it will match employee contributions. For example, one common formula is that employers will match 50% of your contribution, up to a maximum of 6% of salary. So for example, if you contribute the maximum 6% of salary to your 401(k) account, your employer will give you 50% of that (3%) as a matching contribution. So you just got a 50% return on your money!

Now here's the problem: about 20% of people who contribute to a 401(k) account don't contribute enough to get the maximum match. Please check with your plan to make sure you are indeed contributing enough to get the maximum match. (A tip: if you were auto-enrolled in your plan when you were hired you likely are not contributing enough to qualify for the maximum matching contribution. Many auto-enrollment plans set the employee initial contribution rate at just 3%, even though the maximum match is based on a 6% employee contribution.)

DO . . .
CONSIDER A ROTH 401(K).

Many retirement plans now offer a Roth 401(k) in addition to the standard traditional 401(k). As with a Roth IRA, the benefit of the Roth 401(k) is that in retirement your withdrawals will be 100% tax-free. Withdrawals from a traditional 401(k) are taxed at your ordinary income-tax rate. Of course, there is a tradeoff. Money you contribute to a Roth 401(k) is made with after-tax dollars. So unlike a traditional 401(k), your contributions will not reduce your taxable income in the year of the contribution. If you are currently in a low tax bracket I highly recommend considering a Roth 401(k), given that the upfront tax break of a traditional 401(k) isn't very valuable to you. If you are in a higher federal tax bracket I would still encourage you to speak to a trusted tax advisor about the benefits of a Roth 401(k). If you have been contributing to a traditional 401(k) for years, putting new contributions in the Roth 401(k) option can be a great way to build tax diversification for retirement. Moreover, once you retire, you can roll over money in a Roth 401(k) into a Roth IRA. Once the money is in a Roth IRA there will be no Required Minimum Distribution (RMD). That can reduce your taxable income in retirement, and keep more of your money growing for your heirs.

DO . . .

CONSIDER AN IRA ROLLOVER IF YOU LEAVE A JOB.

Once you leave a job you typically have three options: As long as your 401(k) account has $5,000 you can leave it with your old employer. Or you may be able to roll over the money into your new employer's plan. The third option is typically my favorite: doing a direct rollover into your own IRA. Here's why: when you invest in an employer-sponsored 401(k), your investment options are typically restricted to a relatively small number of mutual funds. When you choose the IRA rollover—any discount brokerage will be happy to help you with the paperwork— you will then have the freedom to invest in thousands of funds, ETFs, or other investments. That means you can build a portfolio of very-low-cost index mutual funds or ETFs. As explained earlier, low fees are a very important tool in building retirement security. If you know for a fact that your old employer plan has terrific low-cost options, then it's okay to stay in that plan after you leave. But if your old plan has funds with above-average fees, I want you to get that money rolled over into an IRA ASAP.

DO . . .

MAKE YOUR IRA ROLLOVER
A DIRECT ROLLOVER.

You can open an IRA rollover account at any discount brokerage firm or mutual fund company. The paperwork is not at all hard—and the company you decide to do business with is going to be eager to help you move your money. The one crucial step is to check the box on your rollover application for a "direct" rollover. What this means is that you will never touch the money yourself. With a direct rollover, the discount brokerage or mutual fund company you are opening your IRA account with will contact your old employer and arrange for the money to be sent directly into your new account. Why go this way? Because if you instead have the money sent to you, you must then get it reinvested in an IRA or other tax-deferred retirement account within 60 days. If you fail to do that, you will owe income tax on the entire withdrawn amount and potentially a 10% withdrawal fee as well. A direct rollover is the only way to go.

DO ...

ROLL OVER MULTIPLE ACCOUNTS INTO ONE ACCOUNT PRIOR TO RETIREMENT.

If you have had a few jobs along the way, you might have more than a few old 401(k)s that you haven't done much with. As mentioned earlier, if any of those plans charge high fees, you should get out of them ASAP, and move your money into a IRA rollover account. Also, as you near retirement, it is doubly important to consolidate your multiple accounts into one account. Not only is it easier to keep track of, but also when you begin to take withdrawals in retirement, it will make so much sense to not have to figure out your Required Minimum Distribution from multiple accounts all over the place.

DO ...

KNOW IF YOU LEAVE SERVICE WHEN YOU ARE AT LEAST 55 YOU WILL NOT OWE THE 10% EARLY WITHDRAWAL PENALTY.

Typically if you make a withdrawal from a 401(k) prior to age 59½ you owe a 10% early withdrawal penalty on top of any income tax (if it is a traditional account). But if you are at least 55 when you leave a job, you can make withdrawals without being subject to the early withdrawal penalty (however, taxes, if any, still apply). It's important to understand that if you roll over your 401(k) into an IRA, any withdrawals made prior to age 59½ will be hit with the early withdrawal penalty. My hope is that you don't need to tap any retirement funds in your 50s, but if you anticipate needing to, then leaving some money in your 401(k) makes sense, rather than doing a rollover. That way, you can make withdrawals as necessary without being hit with the 10% early withdrawal penalty.

DON'T . . .
CASH OUT WHEN YOU LEAVE YOUR JOB.

When you leave a job you have the option of cashing out your 401(k). I can't think of a worse move. Yet people with a relatively small amount of money, say $5,000 or so, often decide to take the cash rather then keep the money growing for retirement. Their thinking is, "Gee, it's only $5,000, and I sure could use that to pay some bills. Or for a vacation." Please listen to me, it's not just $5,000. If you keep that $5,000 growing for another 30 years and earn an average of 6%, the $5,000 will be worth nearly $29,000. Besides, if you cash out you will owe income tax if the money was in a traditional 401(k) account. And if you are younger than 55, you will also owe a 10% early withdrawal penalty. So the $5,000 cash out is probably going to net you less than $3,500, compared to nearly $30,000 if the money remains invested for another 30 years. Please, do not ever cash out money that you have diligently saved for retirement.

DON'T . . .

OVER-INVEST IN COMPANY STOCK.

If you work for a company that is public, your matching contribution may be made in company stock. You also may have company stock as an investment option you can choose. Be very careful. No single stock, not even an employer's stock you think has a fantastic future, should ever be more than 10% of your investment portfolio. In fact, I would recommend keeping any single stock to just 5% or so of your investment portfolio. Why? Because no one can ever know with absolute certainty what the future holds for any single stock. If you have most of your money invested in company stock—as many employees of WorldCom and Enron did—you could see the value of your retirement savings wiped out. Diversification is the key.

PART 4

INDIVIDUAL RETIREMENT ACCOUNTS (IRAS)

DO ...

CONSIDER A ROTH IRA.

There are two basic types of IRAs: a traditional IRA and a Roth IRA.

With a traditional IRA you may be eligible to deduct the amount of your annual contribution from your taxable income. So for example, if you contribute $5,500 to a traditional IRA you may be able to reduce your taxable income on your federal tax return by $5,500. When you reach retirement age and begin to take withdrawals, all money you take out will be taxed as ordinary income.

With a Roth IRA there is no upfront tax break; your contribution amount can't be used to reduce your taxable income for that tax year. But in retirement your withdrawals will be 100% tax-free. Moreover, even before retirement you will have easier access to your money. All contributions to a Roth IRA can be withdrawn at any time, regardless of your age or how long the money has been in there, without any tax or early withdrawal penalty. Only the earnings on the money you contributed can be taxed or hit with an early withdrawal penalty. I never recommend pulling money out of any retirement account before retirement, but I think the flexibility of a Roth can be very valuable if you are faced with a serious emergency.

Another important feature of a Roth IRA is that you will not be forced to take distributions once you reach age 70½. With a traditional IRA and a traditional 401(k), the federal government insists you take Required Minimum Distributions (RMDs) so it can collect the income tax you owe on that money. Even if you don't need the money, you still must make your RMD and pay income tax. With a Roth IRA there is no RMD. For families that expect to leave money to heirs, a Roth IRA is smarter than a traditional IRA.

DO . . .

SET UP AN AUTOMATIC DEPOSIT INTO YOUR IRA ACCOUNT.

While the annual maximum contribution to an IRA is $5,500 in 2014 ($6,500 if you are at least 50 years old) that does not mean you must invest that sum all at once. One of the best ways to save in an IRA is to set up automatic periodic transfers from a checking or savings account into your IRA. Every company that offers an IRA will offer automatic deposits free of charge. So for example, you could choose to have $458.33 a month sent to your IRA account; that will total $5,500 over the course of the year. If your goal is to save $6,500, your monthly automatic transfer should be $541.66. I am encouraging you to aim for this annual maximum, but please understand, most discount brokerages and fund companies will be happy to set up an ongoing automatic investing plan that requires just $100 a month.

DO ...

INVEST IN A ROTH IRA AFTER YOU HAVE MAXED OUT ON A 401(K) MATCH.

I always want you to invest enough in a 401(k) that offers a matching contribution to qualify for the maximum match. But I don't want you to automatically invest *more* than that in a traditional 401(k). I think it is smart to also save in a Roth IRA. Here's my strategy:

1. Contribute to your 401(k) up to the point that will qualify you for the maximum employer matching contribution.

2. Then focus on funding a Roth IRA.

3. If you are able to invest more than the annual Roth IRA contribution, then it is okay to go back and invest more in your 401(k).

TIP #1:

If you do not have a retirement plan at work, or your employer does not offer a matching contribution, start with Step 2: Fund your Roth IRA first.

TIP #2:

If you're using a Roth 401(k) at work—and you get an employer match—there's no need to follow the steps I just outlined. You can just do all your investing in the Roth 401(k) and skip the Roth IRA.

For 2014 here are the contribution limits for 401(k)s and IRAs:

401(k):
- $17,500 if you are younger than age 50.
- $23,000 if you are 50 or older.

IRA:
- $5,500 if you are younger than age 50.
- $6,500 if you are 50 or older.

DON'T . . .

INVEST IN A VARIABLE ANNUITY IN YOUR IRA.

Any financial advisor who tells you it is smart to buy a variable annuity for your IRA is not to be trusted. A variable annuity is a tax-deferred investment. Your IRA is also a tax-deferred investment. It makes no sense to buy a tax-deferred investment and then put it inside an IRA. The only one who "wins" is the advisor who no doubt pockets a hefty commission for selling you the variable annuity.

PART 5

PENSIONS

DO . . .

WORK WITH A TRUSTED
FINANCIAL ADVISOR.

Though pensions have become very rare in private-sector jobs, many public-sector workers have a pension. The way most pensions work is that you will have two options: You can take a one-time lump sum payout when you retire and then be responsible for investing that money and making it last through your retirement. Or you can choose an annuity: you will receive a check every month. The annuity check is based on the value of your account (and age) when you retire. Which is best? That is a very personal decision. I encourage you to work with a trusted financial advisor who can help you understand both options.

DO . . .

OPT FOR THE LUMP SUM PAYMENT
IF YOUR GOAL IS TO LEAVE MONEY TO HEIRS.

If you don't anticipate needing the pension money to support yourself in retirement, you should consider the lump sum option; the money can be invested for your heirs. When you opt for an annuity payout, the payments stop once you, or your spouse, die (more on this below).

DO . . .

ROLL OVER YOUR MONEY INTO AN IRA
IF YOU CHOOSE THE LUMP SUM.

If you opt for the lump sum payout, be sure to have the payment directly sent into an IRA rollover account you set up at a discount brokerage or fund company. If you fail to do this, the entire sum will be taxed at the time you receive the money. That's a huge mistake.

DO . . .

TAKE THE 100% JOINT-AND-SURVIVOR BENEFIT IF YOU ARE MARRIED AND CHOOSE THE ANNUITY.

If you decide the annuity benefit is best, you will then be asked to choose what type of annuity payout you want. The two most common payout options are single-life-only and joint-and-survivor. With single-life-only, payments are made to the retiree; when the retiree dies, no beneficiary will receive a payout. With joint-and-survivor, the annuity will be paid to the retiree; if the retiree dies first, the surviving spouse will continue to receive the annuity payment. The joint-and-survivor option will give you a lower monthly payout than if you opted for single-life-only, but I can't stress enough that your focus needs to be on the financial security of the surviving spouse. Here's the basic question you must ask yourself: If you take single-life-only, will the surviving spouse have enough in other income sources to make up for the loss of this payout if the worker/retiree dies first?

DO ...

OPT FOR THE 100% SURVIVOR BENEFIT FOR A JOINT-AND-SURVIVOR ANNUITY PAYOUT.

When you choose the joint-and-survivor option for an annuity option, you have one more decision to make: Do you want the survivor benefit to be 50%, 75%, or 100% of the original payout? As you can imagine, opting for a 50% survivor benefit means the initial benefit (when both spouses are alive) will be higher. That said, I think it is a big mistake to choose the 50% or 75% survivor benefit. It's important to think about what the surviving spouse will have to live on. Could he or she get by with a 50% reduction in this pension payout? The 100% joint-and-survivor benefit ensures the surviving spouse has the highest income possible.

DON'T ...

TAKE THE SINGLE-LIFE-BENEFIT ANNUITY WITH THE GOAL OF BUYING LIFE INSURANCE.

If an advisor recommends you take the single-life annuity and then take part of that higher payment and invest it in life insurance to benefit the surviving spouse, stop working with that advisor. That strategy benefits the advisor who is looking forward to pocketing a fat commission on selling you that life insurance policy.

DON'T . . .

LET A FINANCIAL ADVISOR TALK YOU INTO TAKING A LUMP SUM THAT IS THEN INVESTED IN AN ANNUITY.

Another sign a financial advisor is not looking out for your best interest is if he or she recommends you take the lump sum payout and then purchase your own annuity. Once again, this is all about the advisor earning a big commission on selling you that annuity. My experience is that the annuity you will get directly from your pension is the better deal.

DO . . .

CHECK THAT YOUR PRIVATE PENSION IS COVERED BY THE PBGC.

If you have a pension from a private-sector company, you want to make sure that in the unlikely event something happens to that company—bankruptcy, for example— your pension payments will still be honored. Money that a company sets aside for future pension payouts must be kept separate from its other operations; you can request a summary plan description (SPD) each year to find out whether your pension plan is in good shape or not. You should also check the SPD to confirm that your company is covered by the federal Pension Benefit Guaranty Corporation (PBGC). Most plans are. In the unlikely event your plan can't make good on payments, the PBGC steps in and covers those payments, up to certain limits. You can learn more at pbgc.gov

PART 6

LONG-TERM CARE INSURANCE

DO . . .

CONSIDER LONG-TERM CARE INSURANCE IN YOUR 50S.

Given our increased longevity and the high expense of at-home or nursing-home care, long-term care (LTC) insurance can be a very crucial piece of a retirement plan. I encourage you to work with an experienced agent of long-term care insurance to explore your options. The ideal time to purchase a policy is in your early 50s. I know that sounds early to start paying an annual premium for something you may not use for two or three decades, if ever. But if you wait until your 60s, you may find that a pre-existing medical condition makes a policy too expensive, or it may mean you will be unable to qualify for coverage.

DO . . .
UNDERSTAND THAT LTC INSURANCE PROVIDES AT-HOME COVERAGE.

You will have great flexibility in how you decide to use your benefits. In addition to helping pay for nursing-home care, approved LTC benefits can be used to pay home health-care providers as well.

DO . . .
CONSIDER PURCHASING SOME COVERAGE.

There is no question that LTC insurance can be expensive. Depending on the coverage options you choose, a policy purchased before age 60 might cost up to $2,500 a year. That said, the cost of a semi-private room in a nursing home could be more than $170,000 in 20 years based on the rate of health-care inflation. While it would bring great peace of mind to buy an LTC policy that gives you a big lifetime benefit, that may not be financially possible. That's okay. Something is always better than nothing. Don't feel bad if you can't afford a policy that would likely cover 100% of your future care costs. If you can afford a policy that might cover 20% or 30% of your future costs, that's great. You are doing what you can to help yourself—and your children— down the line.

DO . . .

PLAN FOR PREMIUM INCREASES.

You may be aware that the LTC insurance industry is going through some growing pains. This is a relatively new type of insurance, and insurance companies have been surprised at the high level of payments they have made on existing accounts. (The low interest rates we have had since the financial crisis have compounded the problem because insurers aren't earning much when they invest policy premiums.) The result is that some insurers have raised their premium rates, sometimes by as much as 40%, in recent years. Just so you know, insurers must ask each state insurance commissioner for permission to raise premiums for existing policyholders, and rates can only be raised for all policyholders across the board. That said, the reality is that there have been some steep premium increases in the past few years. My recommendation is to only purchase a policy today that you could still afford even if the premium were to rise 30% to 40%.

DO ...
CONSIDER A POLICY
WITH INFLATION COVERAGE.

We all know that the cost of health services has been rising at a rapid rate for many years. Given that you will likely not be making a claim on your LTC policy for 20 or more years—if ever—it is smart to have your coverage increase each year to help you keep pace with rising costs. This is called an inflation rider. For example, you can choose a policy that will increase your coverage by 4% or 5% a year.

DON'T . . .

BUY A POLICY YOU CAN'T AFFORD.

Stand in your truth: It makes no sense to purchase a policy if you can't afford the premiums. I have heard from too many couples that purchased coverage and then stopped payments a few years later. Please follow my earlier advice: it is better to purchase less coverage if that is what is affordable. Your goal is to be able to keep paying the premiums for at least 25 to 30 years.

DON'T . . .

AUTOMATICALLY CANCEL A POLICY IF YOU CAN'T AFFORD A PREMIUM INCREASE.

If you are confronted with a proposed premium hike that is just too high to cover, please consider other options before you cancel the policy. Sit down with your LTC insurance agent and discuss how you might reduce your policy coverage so the premium does not rise to an uncomfortable level. You have many options: you can reduce the inflation rider or the amount of coverage. Or you may change the elimination period—the weeks where you pay for your care before the policy kicks in.

I also encourage you to sit down with your adult children and explain the situation to them. They may all want to help you pay the additional premium so you can keep the coverage. That will likely be far less of a financial burden to them than the prospect of having to help you pay for care costs out of pocket as you age. Please listen to me: If you love your children, you will consider asking them for help. You are actually doing them a favor if you take the steps to keep your LTC policy active.

PART 7

SOCIAL SECURITY

DO ...

UNDERSTAND SOCIAL SECURITY IS AN INCREDIBLY VALUABLE INFLATION-ADJUSTED ANNUITY.

Your 401(k) doesn't automatically grow risk-free at the rate of inflation. Even if you're lucky enough to have an old-fashioned pension, it doesn't come with inflation protection. You could buy an annuity that includes an annual inflation rider, but that is going to cost you more. Your Social Security retirement benefit, on the other hand, does indeed come with an automatic and 100% free inflation adjustment. Every year there is inflation, benefits are increased. That makes Social Security one of your best retirement tools, and knowing how to maximize this valuable benefit is crucial.

DO ...

WAIT UNTIL YOU REACH FULL RETIREMENT AGE TO START SOCIAL SECURITY.

Everyone is eligible to begin taking their Social Security retirement benefit at age 62. My advice: Don't! The way Social Security works is that we all have a Full Retirement Age (FRA). That is somewhere between age 66 and age 67, based on the year you were born. (If you don't know your FRA, go to ssa.gov.) When you begin your retirement benefit at your FRA, you are entitled to 100% of your earned benefit. If you opt to start your benefit before your FRA, you will receive just 70% to 75% of your FRA benefit. Put another way: at age 62 your benefit is reduced by 25% to 30% of what you are entitled to if you til your FRA. Unless you have a medical condition that makes it unlikely you will live into your 80s, it can be far smarter to wait to begin your benefit.

Focus on the real goal: to make sure you have as much money as possible for what could be a long life. Waiting to age 66/67 to start your Social Security benefit ensures you a much bigger benefit for the rest of your life. (That said, if you absolutely can't find other income sources to cover your living costs between age 62 and age 66/67, then of course you should consider an earlier Social Security benefit. But if you can delay, do it!)

DO . . .

CONSIDER HAVING THE HIGH-INCOME EARNER IN YOUR HOUSEHOLD WAIT UNTIL AGE 70 TO START TAKING SOCIAL SECURITY RETIREMENT BENEFITS.

Okay, we just reviewed that there is a 25% to 30% bonus if you delay beginning your retirement benefit from age 62 to your FRA. Now here's another wrinkle: If you wait until age 70 to start taking your Social Security retirement benefit, that payout will be 24%

to 30% higher than what you're entitled to at your FRA. If you want to leave the highest possible benefit to the surviving spouse, the higher earner should aim to delay claiming until age 70. The other spouse can begin to claim earlier, and the higher earner can even take a spousal benefit before age 70. You can learn more at the AARP website: www.aarp.org/work/social-security. This is such an important retirement planning decision, I highly recommend sitting down with a financial advisor who has expertise in Social Security claiming issues, to fully understand your options.

DON'T ...

THINK YOU CAN EARN MORE TAKING YOUR BENEFIT EARLY AND INVESTING IT.

A common comment I hear when I recommend delaying when you start Social Security payouts is that you can do better taking the lower benefit at age 62 and then invest the money yourself. No. You. Can't. From age 62 to age 66/67 the annual benefit increase is more than 5%. That's 5% guaranteed risk-free. There is no risk-free investment that offers you such a high payout. As I write this, a 10-year Treasury note pays 3% interest. Sure you might be able to earn more than 5% investing in stocks, but what if you don't? Stocks are never a good investment for money you need in less than 10 years. Stocks are risky. The increased payout for delaying when you start Social Security is risk-free.

DON'T . . .
LISTEN TO THE FEARMONGERS.

You have probably heard that Social Security is going to run out of money. I would like you listen to the facts. If we do nothing to "fix" the current system, it is scheduled to run into trouble in 2034. Notice I didn't say "run out of money." The truth is that what will happen—again if we do nothing to fix it before then—is that the program will be able to pay out just 75% or so of promised benefits. Read that again: 75%. Not 0%. Is a 25% reduction a big deal? Of course it is. But the fearmongers want you to think you will not get a penny. That's just irresponsible. What we should all hope for is that our lawmakers can come together and find acceptable tweaks to the program— it does not require a massive overhaul—to ensure the program is solvent for many more generations.

PART 8
LIVING IN RETIREMENT

DO . . .
AIM TO LIVE MORTGAGE-FREE IN RETIREMENT.

Always make it your goal to live mortgage-free once you retire. Either plan to have your current mortgage paid off before you stop working, or plan on selling your home and downsizing to something you can afford without a mortgage. Removing this large monthly cost will give you so much peace of mind in retirement.

DON'T . . .
BE TOO CONSERVATIVE WITH YOUR INVESTMENTS AS YOU NEAR RETIREMENT.

As I explained earlier in this chapter, your retirement years could stretch into three decades. To make sure your money outlasts you, consider keeping a portion of your investments in stocks once you are retired. Not a lot.

But some. Again, the *100-minus-your-age* rule of thumb works here. So at age 70 maybe you have 30% invested in stocks, which over the long-term have the highest likelihood of producing inflation-beating gains.

DO . . .

CONSIDER DIVIDEND-PAYING STOCKS.

Some public companies pay shareholders a dividend a few times a year. The types of companies that pay dividends tend to be large established firms with a long track record of success. That's just the sort of company retirees should focus on: you want reliable over flashy. Now that's not to say that companies that pay dividends won't see their stocks decline in down markets. All stocks fall in bad markets. But dividend-paying stocks typically hold on better. And if you stick with high-quality firms, they should be able to keep paying their dividends even in down markets. This is what I call being "paid to wait." That is, you are getting paid while you wait for stocks to rebound.

Following my earlier advice to be diversified and focus on fees, I recommend learning more about low-cost exchange traded funds (ETFs) that focus on dividend-paying stocks. The SPDR S&P Dividend ETF (Ticker symbol: SDY) and Schwab US Dividend Equity ETF (SCHD) are two options to research.

DO . . .

CONSIDER A BOND LADDER.

For the bond portion of your investments, creating a ladder can be a smart way to deal with today's challenging market environment. As explained earlier, bond interest rates are relatively low today. We don't know exactly when, but at some juncture in the future, rates will rise. And when interest rates rise, bond prices fall. The longer a bond's maturity date, the more sensitive it will be to changes in interest rates.

My recommendation is to focus on bonds with maturities no greater than five or so years. Longer-term bonds will have steeper price declines when rates rise. A bond ladder means you own bonds with varying maturities. For example, you might consider keeping one-third of your bond portfolio in bonds that mature in 1–2 years, another third that matures in 3–4 years, and the final third maturing in 5 or so years. The advantage is that you will earn more interest than if you had 100% invested in one- and two-year bonds. And if, as expected, rates rise as your bonds reach maturity, you will be able to reinvest them in higher-rate bonds. You can build a ladder of Treasury issues with different maturities at the treasurydirect.gov website. Below I have advice for how to build ladders for corporate and municipal bonds.

DO . . .

BE CAREFUL WITH BOND FUNDS.

I have to tell you that I prefer individual bonds to bond funds. With individual bonds the money you invest—your principal—will be repaid in full when the bond matures, assuming the bond issuer did not run into financial trouble. (Sticking with government or high-quality corporate or municipal bonds is how you steer clear of that.)

There is no such set maturity date with a traditional bond fund. So when you go to sell your shares, they may be for less than your initial investment. That said, I understand that funds are the most cost-effective way for you to build a diversified bond portfolio, and are often your only choice when investing in a 401(k). So if you are using bond funds, please make sure the average duration—a measure of how the fund will respond when rates rise—is no more than five years or so. Any longer and you are taking on too much risk for when rates rise in my opinion. Every fund's duration should be clearly displayed on its website, or you should call customer service.

I also encourage you to check out a new breed of bond ETFs that own a pool of bonds that all mature in the same year. Guggenheim's Corporate BulletShares ETFs offer portfolios that mature in 2014, 2016, 2017, and so on, all the way through 2022. So you can effectively build a ladder using these ETFs. They also have another series of high-yield corporate bonds that start in 2014 and go all the way through 2020. Please be careful here: High-yield bonds are what is known as junk bonds. Yes, they pay you more income, but in down markets they experience steep losses akin to stock losses. The Corporate BulletShares series is the better choice for traditional bond investments, as it owns high-grade issues. iShares has also launched a similar series of fixed-maturity ETFs. The iSharesBonds Corporate Term ETFs include portfolios maturing in 2016, 2018, 2020, and 2023.

DO . . .

TAKE YOUR REQUIRED
MINIMUM DISTRIBUTIONS (RMDS) ON TIME.

The federal government insists you begin to take money out of your traditional IRAs and 401(k)s in the year you turn 70½. (The specific rule is that you can delay your first withdrawal until April 1 of the calendar year following when you turn 70½.) Why? Because the government wants to collect the income tax on those withdrawals, regardless of whether you need the money or not. If you do not follow the RMD rules, you can face a 50% tax on the amount you should have withdrawn.

The company where you have your retirement accounts invested will help you determine your RMD. Again, this is why I recommend keeping your retirement accounts at the same discount brokerage or fund company. It will make calculating your RMDs all the easier.

An important tip: You do not need to take RMDs from each retirement account. Once you determine the total RMD you must take in a given year, it can come out of just one account. So for example, if you have a 401(k) that is paying a terrific interest rate on the stable value fund, don't take money out of that account if you can satisfy your RMD with withdrawals from other retirement accounts.

DO . . .
CREATE A SUSTAINABLE WITHDRAWAL PLAN.

I think we can agree the biggest goal of living comfortably in retirement is to make sure you don't run out of money! That requires establishing a smart rate of withdrawal when you begin to take distributions, and then revisiting your plan periodically to make sure you are still in great shape. This is where a trusted financial advisor can be a huge asset; he or she can run the numbers for you and keep you on track.

For example, one rule of thumb is that you might start your withdrawal rate at 4%, and then adjust that sum for inflation in subsequent years. But if you wait until age 70 to begin withdrawals, you may be able to set a slightly higher initial withdrawal rate. Conversely, if you happen to retire right when we are in a down or bear market for stocks, you may need to consider a lower initial withdrawal rate. I cannot stress enough how a trusted financial advisor can help you run the numbers and develop a smart plan that you monitor throughout your retirement.

DO ...
CONSIDER PART-TIME WORK.

If you are concerned about your money lasting throughout your retirement, why not consider some part-time work? I am not talking about a nose-to-the-grindstone career job, but rather, a more low-key job that serves two purposes. Having some extra income is obviously helpful. But studies have shown that people who stay engaged in some sort of work—especially something they enjoy—are often happier in retirement.

DO . . .
CHECK YOUR RETIREMENT ACCOUNT BENEFICIARIES.

If you're honest, I bet it has been years since you last reviewed the beneficiaries on your retirement accounts. Don't assume that what you have in your will or trust will take care of things. It won't with your retirement accounts; you need to make sure the beneficiary designations for those accounts are up to date.

DON'T . . .
STAY IN A HOME THAT YOU CAN'T HONESTLY AFFORD.

Even if you have the mortgage paid off before you retire, please seriously consider if you can afford the property tax, insurance, and maintenance costs for that home on your fixed income. It is far better to move to a more affordable home early in your retirement (or preferably before you retire) than to try and hang on for as long as possible and then in your 80s or 90s be forced to move because the home is too expensive for you to maintain.

DON'T . . .

TAKE OUT A REVERSE MORTGAGE IN YOUR 60s.

Age 62 is the earliest you can apply for a reverse mortgage. If you're planning on applying that young I have to tell you that the better move is to consider selling the home and reducing your living costs by moving to a less expensive area and home.

So many people have run into trouble defaulting on their reverse mortgages that the federal government changed the rules in late 2013. There are now lower limits on what you can borrow, and how much you can tap in the first year. The big problem is that so many people with reverse mortgages couldn't keep up with their property tax and insurance. Under new rules you may be required to deposit money in a special escrow account to cover your ongoing tax and insurance costs. Again, if you find yourself in that situation, I would take it as a signal that you should consider downsizing.

DON'T . . .
INVEST IN LONG-TERM BOND FUNDS.

Ever since the financial crisis, retirees have faced a very tough time finding safe, reliable sources of income. That can make long-term bonds look enticing. The longer the maturity of a bond, the higher the interest payment. But remember, the longer the bond's term, the more its price will fall when interest rates rise. That is, longer-term bonds are riskier than shorter-term bonds when interest rates rise. As I have explained, no one knows exactly when rates will rise, but as I write this in early 2014, rates are still below their historic norms. The long-term trend is for rates to rise, not fall.

We had a small preview of what might lie ahead in 2013: From May to September, interest rates rose 1.3 percentage points. During that time, short-term bond funds fell an average of 1.3%, intermediate-term bond funds fell 5%, and long-term bond funds lost nearly 9%.

DON'T . . .
GET FOOLED BY JUNK BONDS.

The bonds from companies that don't have pristine balance sheets are called junk bonds. To compensate investors, issuers of junk bonds pay a higher yield. That can look very enticing to retirees in search of income. In early 2014, the average junk mutual fund (also known as a high-yield corporate bond fund) had a yield of more than 6%, compared to 3% or so for funds that invest in high-quality corporate issues and government issues.

But be careful. Junk bonds behave more like stocks than bonds. When we hit a rough patch, junk bonds can have steep loses. Consider what happened in 2008: The average junk bond fund lost more than 25%. Meanwhile, an index of high-quality corporate and government issues gained 5%. My recommendation is that if you want some income from junk bonds, that money should come from your stock allocation, given how risky this investment can be.

Protecting Your Family

PART 1

THE MUST-HAVE DOCUMENTS

DO . . .

HAVE A WILL.

You absolutely, positively need a will. Without a will or any other estate-planning document in place, when you die your assets will be disbursed following your state's laws for such situations. That's what is known as dying intestate. It doesn't matter what you told a loved one, or if you wrote down your wishes on a piece of paper. Without a will, the state follows its own intestate rules.

DO . . .

REALIZE YOU PROBABLY NEED
A REVOCABLE LIVING TRUST AS WELL.

Wills are the bare minimum in terms of estate-planning documents. Even if you have a will, there is a good chance that when you pass, your heirs will have to wait for your will to wend its way through the probate court process. Only very small estates, typically valued at less than $100,000, can avoid the full probate process.

It can take months for a will to be approved by a probate judge. And you will likely need to hire a lawyer to help you make your way through the process. That can become expensive, depending on the particulars of your situation.

All of that can be avoided if you also have a revocable living trust; with a trust, your estate will not need to go through probate. And as I explain below, there is another important reason you should have a trust.

DO . . .

RELAX.
YOU ARE IN CHARGE OF YOUR REVOCABLE
LIVING TRUST, AND IT CAN BE CHANGED.

Okay, I know you might be thinking, "Aren't trusts just for the super wealthy?" Absolutely not! They are for anyone who has some assets—a home, investments—they want passed on to their heirs with the least fuss and muss.

While you are alive, you will be the trustee of your trust. That means you're in charge. The trust can be adjusted at any time. That's what revocable means: If you change your mind about some stipulation in your trust, you can change it.

DO . . .
FUND THE TRUST.

A trust is like an empty piece of luggage. You need to pack your trust with all your assets. This is what is called "funding your trust." It involves having the title to your assets—such as any property, or life insurance policies—switched to your trust. So for example, instead of Jane

Doe taking title to her home as Jane Doe, she would make her trust the owner. The title would be Jane Doe trustee for the Jane Doe living trust. If you already own an asset, you need to go through the paperwork of changing the title. Or you can hire a lawyer to take care of the funding.

DO ...
ADD AN INCAPACITY CLAUSE
TO YOUR REVOCABLE LIVING TRUST.

Another great reason to have a trust is because it can help you and your loved ones while you are alive. As its name implies, a living trust is in force during your lifetime. A will, on the other hand, only lays out your wishes for *after* you pass.

So why do you need a trust during your lifetime? I know this is not the most cheerful topic, but I want you to think about the possibility that at some point you may not be able to communicate your desires, or you may not be able to handle your financial matters. I've been through this with loved ones, and I imagine many of you have as well. It is not an easy passage. But a revocable living trust can make it far less arduous for you and your loved ones.

You want to make sure your trust includes an incapacity clause. This means that if and when you are no longer able to handle your affairs, the incapacity clause will kick into action and a person you have designated will step in and tend to your affairs on your behalf. Paying your bills, overseeing your investments. Making sure the taxes get paid. You will appoint that person when you set up your trust; this is something you can do today to make sure that if and when the time ever comes, your loved ones will have an easy path to continuing to care for you when you need their assistance.

DO . . .

CREATE A DURABLE POWER OF ATTORNEY FOR HEALTH CARE.

If you become too ill to express your wishes to your medical team, wouldn't it relieve you greatly to know—right here and now while you are healthy—that someone you love will have the legal backing to speak for you? The person you appoint as your durable power of attorney for health care will act as your proxy or agent and communicate to your doctors what your wishes are.

DO ...
CREATE AN ADVANCE DIRECTIVE.

This essential document will help guide the person you designate as your health care agent with end-of-life decisions. Look, I get it. Reading that sentence might have made you squirm a little. So many of us don't want to think about dying. But I ask you with an open heart to consider this: What if you become too ill to speak for yourself, and your loved ones don't know what it is you do or don't want in terms of intervention? Or even worse, what if you have not made your wishes clear and your loved ones can't agree on what you would want? Doesn't thinking about *that* scenario make you squirm even more? With an advance directive in place, you can ensure that your wishes will be followed, and you can stop wrenching family arguments before they even start.

DO ...
REVIEW YOUR RETIREMENT-PLAN AND LIFE-INSURANCE BENEFICIARIES.

Your inheritance preferences that you lay out in your trust don't apply to your 401(k), IRA, and other retirement assets. With those accounts the money will be disbursed at your death according to the beneficiary designation on file with the plan. Can't remember filing out that form? That's exactly my point! You may have done this years ago and not updated it as your life evolved. For example, if you never removed your ex-spouse as the beneficiary of your 401(k), when you pass your ex is entitled to the account. It doesn't matter what your divorce decree says or what you have spelled out in your trust. The beneficiary document on file with the retirement plan is what matters.

Life insurance works the same way. The beneficiary of the policy is entitled to the death benefit, regardless of what you say in the trust document.

Please review all your beneficiary designations and make sure they reflect your current wishes.

DON'T . . .

ASSUME A WILL IS ALL YOU NEED.

As explained earlier, a will is likely not sufficient. Even if you have a small estate that could avoid probate, a revocable living trust will make it much easier for a loved one to step in and manage your affairs during your lifetime, if you become unable to oversee matters.

DON'T ...

ASSUME SOMEONE WILL BE YOUR DURABLE POWER OF ATTORNEY FOR HEALTH CARE OR EXECUTOR.

Ask. A person you love deeply, and who loves you deeply, may not be the best person to act as your health care agent. You should never assume that you can just appoint anyone to this role to oversee the disposition of your estate when you die (that's what an executor does). You need to ask the person if they are comfortable taking on that role.

Once you do have both your durable power of attorney for health care and your executor squared away, I encourage you to tell other family members. Better everyone get on board now, when you are healthy and able to answer any questions or concerns they may have.

DON'T ...

MISTAKENLY DISINHERIT KIDS IF YOU REMARRY.

If you remarry and you intend to leave assets acquired prior to your remarriage to children (or anyone else) other than your new spouse, you need to be especially careful with your estate and title documents. The key is how you title assets with your new spouse. If you opt for joint tenancy with right of survivorship, that means your spouse automatically takes possession of your share of the asset when you pass. Even if in your trust you make it clear you want a child to inherit your home (or your share of the home), the title overrides the trust. If you are a blended family, I highly recommend you and your spouse work with an estate-planning attorney who specializes in blended family situations to make sure everything will eventually be disbursed as you intend.

PART 2

LIFE INSURANCE

DO . . .

PROTECT ANYONE DEPENDENT ON YOUR INCOME.

Life insurance is one of those topics that is needlessly presented as being very complicated, very expensive, and thus, very anxiety inducing. Relax. It's really quite simple.

Here's all you need to consider: Is anyone dependent on your income? A child? A spouse? An elderly parent? If the answer is yes, then you need life insurance. If no one relies on your income then you don't need life insurance.

DO . . .
FOCUS ON TERM LIFE INSURANCE.

If you just answered yes to the previous question, your next step is to figure out what type of insurance you need. This is where the anxiety kicks in. There are so many different types of life insurance, and the last thing you want to deal with is a pushy agent shoving all sorts of confusing charts in your face to convince you she has the perfect solution for you. I get why buying life insurance is such a hard step for many to take.

I am going to make it very simple for you. The vast majority of people should buy term life insurance.

As its name implies, term life insurance is active for a set period of time; the term. A typical term can be 10 years or 20 years. At the end of the term, your policy lapses and there is no more coverage. Sound risky? Not in the least. I want you to think about who is dependent on your income. Chances are it is young children. If you were to die while they are minors, you certainly want to make sure there is a payout from a life insurance policy to take care of them until they are adults. Is that forever? No! Chances are a 20-year term policy is all you would need, right?

If your spouse is dependent on your income, chances are that as you age, you will have other assets that will support your spouse: investments, retirement accounts, real estate, etc. Typically it is young couples that should have life insurance. But that's not a permanent need. After 10 or 20 years you will likely not need life insurance as you have accumulated other assets.

Term insurance is the way to go when you only need to protect loved ones for a specific period of time. (If someone will be dependent on your income in perpetuity—for example, a special-needs child or sibling—then you will want to discuss alternative life-insurance choices with an insurance agent.)

DO ...

PURCHASE LIFE INSURANCE FOR A STAY-AT-HOME PARENT.

It's not just the income earner who needs a policy. I want you to consider this scenario for a moment: If your partner is a stay-at-home parent, ask yourself what would happen if he or she dies unexpectedly? I know that's not easy to ponder, but it is vitally important for your family's financial security, so please stick with me here. Chances are you would need to hire help just to deal with the logistics of getting young children to/from school and after-school activities. Can you imagine running the household by yourself? My guess is you will be consumed with parenting, and not have the time to handle all the household upkeep and chores. That's where a life insurance policy on a stay-at-home parent becomes so important. It will give you the money to hire support staff.

DO ...

AIM FOR A DEATH BENEFIT THAT IS 25 TIMES YOUR DEPENDENTS' INCOME NEEDS.

One of the big questions you need to answer is: How much life insurance do you need? The amount is known as the death benefit. This is the amount of money that will be paid to your beneficiaries when you die. My advice is to determine the annual income needs for your dependents and then multiply that sum by 25. So if your dependents need $50,000 a year, you would want a term insurance policy that has a $1.25 million death benefit.

Why so much? Your goal is to make sure your loved ones don't have to worry about money. If your death benefit is just one or two years' worth of their living expenses, they will need to dig into that immediately. So after a year or two, the money is gone. What are they going to do after that?

By purchasing a policy with a death benefit that is 25 times their income needs, you are setting them up for life. With that large payout, they can invest the money conservatively, say in high-quality tax-free bonds, and live off of the income. They will not need to eat into the principal. For example, a $1.25 million death benefit that is invested in municipal bonds and earns 4% interest will generate $50,000 in annual tax-free income. So you've addressed their income needs, and they still have the $1.25 million principal to keep generating income for them for years to come.

When you shop for term life insurance, I think you will be surprised how affordable it can be. A 20-year term life insurance policy with a $1.25 million death benefit for a 40-year old in good health should cost around $1,000 a year. That's less than $85 a month to know your loved ones will be financially okay if you were to die prematurely. Accuquote.com and Selectquote.com are two solid companies that sell term life insurance from multiple insurers.

DO ...

BUY A GUARANTEED LEVEL TERM POLICY.

With a guaranteed policy, the premium never changes. It will be the same the first year as it is the last year of your policy.

DO ...

MAKE SURE THAT YOU HAVE TERM LIFE INSURANCE IN PLACE TILL YOUR YOUNGEST CHILD IS 23 YEARS OF AGE.

If you anticipate your children will go to college, ensuring there is income through their early 20s makes it more likely they will be able to get a degree with a manageable amount of student loans, if any.

DON'T . . .

LET AN AGENT TALK YOU INTO WHOLE LIFE OR OTHER "PERMANENT" INSURANCE.

Many life insurance agents don't like term insurance. Simply because it is so inexpensive, the commission they earn isn't worth much. For agents who rely on a commission, you can imagine they are going to be inclined to push policies with higher commissions. These policies all fall under the umbrella of permanent insurance, in that the policy never runs out; there is no finite term. Again, ask yourself: Do you really need life insurance forever? Chances are the answer is no. So that's the first reason to be suspicious of anyone telling you permanent insurance is the way to go.

The next thing an agent will tell you about a permanent policy is that it is a great investment. You will invariably be shown a chart with all the "cash value" you could have in years to come.

Please listen to me carefully: It makes no sense to buy life insurance for its purported investment value. What the agent doesn't tell you is that the cost of buying a so-called cash-value life insurance policy is going to be much higher than a term policy. The annual premium can be 8 to 10 times more than a term policy. That makes for a far better commission for the agent, but it is not in any way a deal for you.

There all sorts of embedded costs to the investment component of a cash-value policy. It makes far more sense to buy an inexpensive term policy and invest on your own in low-cost mutual funds and exchange traded funds (ETFs).

DON'T ...
CANCEL AN OLD POLICY UNTIL THE NEW POLICY IS IN FORCE.

If you have an expensive cash-value policy that you are considering replacing with a term insurance policy, please be very careful. Never cancel a policy before the replacement policy is approved and you have made the first premium payment.

DON'T ...
MAKE A MINOR CHILD THE BENEFICIARY OF YOUR LIFE INSURANCE POLICY.

Minors are not allowed to inherit money directly. If you mistakenly have your child as your life insurance beneficiary, the court will not allow the money to be released to the child or the child's guardian. The court becomes the overseer of the money. That's not what anybody wants. Life insurance should be owned (titled) with your revocable living trust as the beneficiary. If you were to die while the policy is in force, the money will be automatically disbursed to the trust. And the successor trustee of the trust will then follow the instructions in the trust as to how that money is to be used.

DON'T . . .
BUY A LIFE INSURANCE POLICY
ON A CHILD.

Let's review the basic reason for life insurance: It is to replace the income you provide dependents. Is anyone dependent on your child for income? Of course not. So it makes little sense to purchase a life insurance for a child as protection for that child. Now I respect that some people want to purchase a life insurance policy on a child so in the tragic event that the child dies before you, you will have sufficient money for a funeral. If that's your concern, then my advice is to buy a 20-year term insurance policy, but with a very small death benefit of $10,000 or so to cover the funeral costs.

Kids and Money

DO . . .

SET THE RIGHT EXAMPLE.

Listen to me, you can say all the right things, but what your children will learn from is your behavior. If they see you making impulse purchases or engaging in retail therapy that is what they will learn. If they see you methodically paying your bills online—and on time—that's what they will grow up thinking is normal.

DO . . .

BE MINDFUL OF HOW YOUR WORDS AND ACTIONS WILL BE INTERPRETED.

Every word you utter as it relates to money is imprinting a strong association with young children. For example, when you are getting ready to go to work and you kiss your child goodbye with the words "I hate to leave you, but Mommy/Daddy needs to go to work to make money," then in your child's mind, money and work are now the enemy.

Another classic way in which you may mindlessly teach the wrong thing is letting your kids push the buttons at the ATM. So they think it's a game!

See how a seemingly innocent decision you make can have a profound impact? You must, at an appropriate age and in an appropriate manner, teach where money really flows from: your hard work.

DO ...

TIE ALLOWANCES TO AGE-APPROPRIATE CONTRIBUTIONS TO THE FAMILY.

Every child from two or three years on should be held responsible for basic actions that are not tied to an allowance. Getting the toys back into the toy box for the young ones. Getting the dishes into/out of the dishwasher for older ones. I will leave the specifics up to you. The point is that everyone in the family has a base level of contributions that are not tied to money in any way. Once you've established those chores, add on a few more that will be the basis for an allowance. Again, you decide on the specifics. Maybe helping with the yard upkeep, or the laundry.

Allowances should be paid at a set time, and there should be a short discussion of how well (or not) the chores were performed that week. Young children should be paid every week. Once you have a teen, consider spreading out the allowance to every two weeks, or monthly, to help teach basic money management. (More on this follows.)

DO . . .
INCLUDE YOUR TEENS IN BILL PAYING.

Telling your children things are expensive is not helpful. Showing them is how they learn. I think it is smart to have your teen join in when you sit down to pay the bills—let them control the mouse if you use online bill pay. It not only opens their eyes to the cost of keeping your household up and running, it becomes a conversation starter about spending and budgeting.

DO . . .
TEACH TEENS TO MANAGE MONEY.

Once your child is a teen, you want to start giving them more responsibility to manage money. Allowances should be handed out every two weeks to give your child the responsibility of making their money last over that entire stretch. By the time they are a junior or senior in high school, I would make the payment monthly, and sit down and talk through how to budget so there is still money in week four! Be encouraging; your energy should be that of a cheerleader. You want your child to feel excited and proud to be given this responsibility.

DO ...

ADD YOUR CHILD TO YOUR CREDIT CARD IF YOU HAVE A SOLID CREDIT SCORE.

You can add a child as an "authorized user" on your account. When you do this your child will begin to build a credit report at the three credit bureaus that will help them establish their own solid credit score. In essence, they will inherit/piggyback on your credit score. If your FICO credit score is 720 or higher this is a smart move; your good score is a great head start for your child. Of course, if you do this, you are to establish guidelines for when they are allowed to use the card.

DO . . .

CONSIDER A 3-TIER APPROACH TO HANDLING MONEY GIFTS.

If your child is given money as gifts, consider establishing a family process for how those gifts will be treated. You must respect that it is your child's money; it is not up to you to micromanage exactly how the money is spent. That said, you can establish guidelines for your child to follow. I think there are three main buckets that gifts should be divided into: Free to Spend, Savings, and Donations. Discuss as a family what percentage should go to each bucket.

FREE TO SPEND: Do not judge or guide. This is your child's decision.

SAVINGS: If the child is under 10, consider dividing the savings money into two buckets: a very short-term goal and one longer-term goal. For example, one goal might be three or six months in the future. That gives a young child something tangible to focus on. The rest should be for a longer-term goal, such as college. The idea here is to make sure you don't turn off a young child to saving by siphoning off all the money for a goal that is so far away that they can't relate. It's not easy to expect a six-year-old to appreciate the need to save for a goal that is 12 years off; that's twice their age!

DONATIONS: Again, do not judge or guide. Let your child decide what charities to contribute to. And have them be an active participant in making the donation. If it is local, make an appointment to stop by and have your child physically make the donation. If they want to give to a national or international charity, have them give you the money and then sit down together at the computer and let them help you make the donation online. You want this to be as tangible an experience as possible.

DO . . .
CREATE AN INCENTIVE TO SAVE.

Consider giving your child a matching contribution for saving for long-term goals that are about needs, not wants. College. Or a used car they want to buy in a few years so they can get a part-time job. So for example, for every dollar your child puts in a savings account, you can add 25 cents. Or 50 cents. It's up to you how much to match.

DO . . .

CONSIDER FUNDING A ROTH IRA FOR A WORKING CHILD.

If your finances are in great shape—you have no credit card debt and are on track with retirement savings—and your child has a paying job, you can help him establish a Roth IRA. While it's asking too much of a 16-year-old with a part-time job to think about retirement in 50 years, you can gift an IRA contribution to your child. The only IRS rule is that anyone with an IRA must have had earned income in the year they contribute to the IRA. But it doesn't matter where the money for the contribution comes from. Let's say your child earns $2,500 this year. If you have the means, you could give your child $2,500 that he could then contribute to his own Roth IRA. A single $2,500 contribution will grow to more than $45,000 over 50 years assuming a 6% annualized rate of return

For parents and grandparents concerned about how to help their kids and grandkids get a leg up, this Roth IRA strategy can help build quite a legacy. And it's not just for teens; this is a great way to help twenty-somethings struggling to pay their bills, let alone save for retirement.

DO ...

EXPECT ADULT CHILDREN LIVING WITH YOU TO CONTRIBUTE TO HOUSEHOLD EXPENSES.

It is increasingly more common for children to move back home after college, or to never leave in the first place. Even if they are making this decision for financial reasons, it is important that they pay you some form of rent or contribute something to household expenses. This is not punishment. It is helping your child begin to live in their truth: they are now an adult. With adult responsibilities. I know this makes some parents bristle. Please listen to me: This is a sign of respect you both convey to each other.

One option is for you to take the money your child pays you each month—yes, it should be once a month on a specific date—and put it in a savings account. No need to mention this to your child. But when she is ready to move out, you can hand her a check—repaying her the money she paid you. You've just jumpstarted your child's emergency fund!

DON'T ...

EVER GIVE AN ALLOWANCE WITHOUT A REASON.

No child deserves an allowance just for being your child. Please. Allowances are to be tied to expectations for how your child contributes to the family.

DON'T ...

EVER GIVE ALLOWANCES FOR GOOD BEHAVIOR OR GOOD GRADES.

Allowances are for actions that exceed your family's core basic expectations. I believe good behavior and good grades are a basic expectation that should never be linked to money or gifts. Just think of the message you are sending.

DON'T ...

PAY FOR YOUR TEEN'S EVERY WANT.

It is your job to provide for their needs, not their wants. Set expectations. Yes, they may need new jeans, but you and I both know that can run you $50 or $150. If they have their heart set on the more expensive version, it's time to get a part-time job. Or to use their gift savings. Will they roll their eyes at you when you lay down the rules? Of course! They are teens. But listen to me: If you cave and just say yes to everything, you are hurting both of you. It hurts you if money you are overspending on your child is money you should be using to pay down debts or build up your retirement savings. And it hurts your child in the long run if you fail the basic parenting responsibility of teaching the value of money and the need to spend money wisely so there is still money to put toward savings. If you don't teach your kids, who will? No one. This is on you, Mom and Dad.

DON'T . . .

SAVE FOR COLLEGE BEFORE YOU HAVE YOUR RETIREMENT SAVINGS ON TRACK.

There is no greater love than what you feel for a child. I get it. And that is why I am telling you that if you love your child, you will make saving for your retirement your priority. There are loans for college. There are no loans for retirement. Close your eyes for a moment and think a few decades into the future; your kids are grown adults. If you have done a great job saving for retirement, your kids will be thrilled; they don't have to worry about helping to support you at a time in their life when they will probably be quite busy raising their own kids. Putting your retirement ahead of their college savings is not selfish. It is an act of love.

DON'T ...

LET YOUR CHILD BORROW FOR COLLEGE WITH A PRIVATE LOAN.

If your child asks you to co-sign for a student loan, be very, very worried. The only loans that require a co-signer are private loans offered by banks. Private loans are too risky for the borrower. And it can be risky for you: signing on means that in the event that your child does not repay the loan, you will be liable for the payments. And these loans are nearly impossible to get rid of in bankruptcy. Your child should choose a school that they can financially afford to attend. I strongly encourage your child to focus on using only federal Stafford loans. They are much better than private student loans. There are limits on how much you can borrow each year through the Stafford program (for specifics, refer to Section 2, Borrow Wise). Their aim should be to attend a school where financial aid plus their Stafford loan would cover their expenses.

A FEW FINAL WORDS

Follow my Do's and Don'ts and you will be on your way to building lasting financial security.

I also want to share with you some of my most treasured beliefs; they have helped me become who I am. I share them with you in the hope they help you create the future you want and deserve.

— SUZE

When you make average great,
your dreams come true.

The less you feel,
the more you spend.

When you undervalue who you are,
the world undervalues what you do.

Trust yourself more
than you trust others.

No one will ever care about your money
as much as you.

Stop spending money you don't have
to impress people you don't even
really know or like.

Want to find the best financial advisor in the world?
Look in the mirror.

Say no out of love versus yes out of fear.

Be proud of who you are,
not ashamed of what you don't have.

A truly wealthy life lies in defining yourself
by who you are, not by what you have.
For in the end you cannot take a penny with you.

True financial harmony is achieved
when your pleasure in saving money equals
your pleasure in spending it.

It is better to do nothing than
to do something you do not understand.

People first, then money, then things.

ABOUT THE AUTHOR

Suze Orman has been called "a force in the world of personal finance" and a "one-woman financial advice powerhouse" by *USA Today*. Orman is a two-time Emmy Award–winning television host, winner of eight Gracie Awards, and author of nine consecutive *New York Times* bestsellers.

Twice named by *Time* magazine as one of the most influential people in the world, Orman has written, produced, and co-hosted eight PBS specials. She is the most successful single fundraiser in the history of PBS. Orman is the financial editor to *O, the Oprah Magazine* and host of the award-winning *The Suze Orman Show*, which is in its 13th year on television.